The Heart of the Woods

 **HARCOURT BRACE JOVANOVICH, PUBLISHERS**
Orlando San Diego Chicago Dallas

The Heart of the Woods

ODYSSEY An HBJ Literature Program
Second Edition

Sam Leaton Sebesta

Consultants

Elaine M. Aoki	Myra Cohn Livingston
Willard E. Bill	Daphne P. Muse
Sonya Blackman	Sandra McCandless Simons
Sylvia Engdahl	Barre Toelken

Acknowledgments

For permission to reprint copyrighted material, grateful acknowledgment is made to the following sources:

Atheneum Publishers: "We Could Be Friends" from *The Way Things Are and Other Poems* by Myra Cohn Livingston (A Margaret K. McElderry Book). Copyright © 1974 by Myra Cohn Livingston. From *Oh, A-Hunting We Will Go* by John Langstaff (A Margaret K. McElderry Book). Text copyright © 1974 by John Langstaff. "Spinning Song" from *Today Is Saturday* by Zilpha Keatley Snyder. Text copyright © 1969 by Zilpha Keatley Snyder. "Something Is There" and "We Three" from *See My Lovely Poison Ivy* by Lilian Moore. Text copyright © 1975 by Lilian Moore.
Bradbury Press, Inc.: Text from *Rrra-ah* by Eros Keith. Copyright © 1969 by Eros Keith.
Shirley Crawford, Kalispel Tribe: First eight lines from "Grandfather" by Shirley Crawford. © 1968 by Shirley Crawford.
Delacorte Press/Seymour Lawrence: "Sebastian and the Monster" excerpted from *Journeys of Sebastian* by Fernando Krahn. Copyright © 1968 by Fernando Krahn.
The Dial Press: "He wears a wooden shirt" and "When they are empty" excerpted from *Three Rolls and One Doughnut: Fables from Russia,* retold by Mirra Ginsburg. Copyright © 1970 by Mirra Ginsburg.
E. P. Dutton: Adapted from *Socks for Supper* by Jack Kent. Copyright © 1978 by Jack Kent. A Parents' Magazine Press Book.
Ernesto Galarza: "Frog," "Earthworm," and "Bee" from *Poemas Pe-que Pe-que Pe-que-nitos (Very Very Short Nature Poems)* by Ernesto Galarza.
Harper & Row, Publishers, Inc.: Art and adapted text from pages 39–54 of *Little Bear's Visit* (Titled: "Grandfather's Story") by Else Holmelund Minarik, illustrated by Maurice Sendak. Text copyright © 1961 by Else Holmelund Minarik. Pictures copyright © 1961 by Maurice Sendak. Text and art from "The Garden" in *Frog and Toad Together,* written and illustrated by Arnold Lobel. Copyright © 1971, 1972 by Arnold Lobel. Adapted and abridged text from *Dinosaur Time* by Peggy Parish. Text copyright © 1974 by Margaret Parish. "Heart of the Woods" by Wesley Curtright from *Golden Slippers,* edited by Arna Bontemps. Copyright 1941 by Harper & Row, Publishers, Inc. Complete art and text from *Pierre: A Cautionary Tale in Five Chapters and a Prologue,* written and illustrated by Maurice Sendak. Copyright © 1962 by Maurice Sendak. Adapted text of *Crystal Is the New Girl* by Shirley Gordon. Text copyright © 1976 by Shirley Gordon. "Rope Rhyme" from *HONEY, I LOVE: And Other Love Poems* by Eloise Greenfield (Thomas Y. Crowell Co.). Copyright © 1978 by Eloise Greenfield. "Snowflakes drift" from *I See the Winds* by Kazue Mizumura. Copyright © 1966 by Kazue Mizumura. "Dilly Dilly Piccalilli" from *Father Fox's Pennyrhymes* by Clyde Watson (Thomas Y. Crowell Co.). Text copyright © 1971 by Clyde Watson.
Holt, Rinehart and Winston, Publishers: "January" (Retitled: "Walk Tall in the World") from *Everett Anderson's Year* by Lucille Clifton. Copyright © 1974 by Lucille Clifton.
Houghton Mifflin Company: "Split Pea Soup," story and pictures, from *George and Martha* by James Marshall. Copyright © 1972 by James Marshall.
Macmillan Publishing Company: Reprint of *Max* by Rachel Isadora. Copyright © 1976 by Rachel Isadora. Adaptation of "The Elves and the Shoemaker" from *Grimm Brothers Household Stories,* translated from the German by Lucy Crane. New York: Macmillan Publishing Company, 1927.

Macmillan Publishing Co., Inc.: "Soft Grass" from *Green Light, Go,* A Bank Street Reader, Revised Edition by Bank Street College of Education. Copyright © 1966, 1972 by Macmillan Publishing Co., Inc.

Eve Merriam, c/o International Creative Management: "Alarm Clock" from *Finding a Poem* by Eve Merriam. Copyright © 1970 by Eve Merriam.

National Textbook Company: "Caballito" from *Mother Goose on the Rio Grande* by Frances Alexander. Copyright © 1973 by National Textbook Company.

Random House, Inc.: Adaptation of "The Trolls and the Pussy Cat" from *Favorite Tales of Monsters and Trolls* by George Jonsen. Copyright © 1977 by Random House, Inc. "The Ant and the Dove" from *Aesop's Fables,* retold by Anne Terry White. Copyright © 1964 by Anne Terry White.

Schroder Music Company (ASCAP): From the song "You Can't Make a Turtle Come Out" from *There's Music in the Air,* words and music by Malvina Reynolds. Copyright © 1962 by Schroder Music Co. (ASCAP).

Charles Scribner's Sons: "At the Top of My Voice" from *At the Top of My Voice and Other Poems* by Felice Holman. Copyright © 1970 by Felice Holman.

The Seabury Press, Inc.: "It has two feet," "A short, short tail," and "Six legs for walking" from *It Does Not Say Meow and Other Animal Riddle Rhymes* by Beatrice Schenk de Regniers. Copyright © 1972 by Beatrice Schenk de Regniers. *The Magic Porridge Pot* retold by Paul Galdone. Copyright © 1976 by Paul Galdone.

The Literary Trustees of Walter de la Mare and The Society of Authors as their representatives: "Some One" from *Collected Poems* by Walter de la Mare.

Margaret Winsor Stubbs: "Solomon Grundy" by Frederick Winsor from *The Space Child's Mother Goose* by Frederick Winsor and Marian Parry. Published by Simon & Schuster, 1958.

Walker & Company: "A Ghost Story" from *The Prancing Pony,* adapted by Charlotte B. DeForest. Copyright © 1968 by Walker & Company.

Albert Whitman & Company: Adapted from *Mary Jo's Grandmother* by Janice May Udry. Text copyright © 1970 by Janice May Udry.

Art Acknowledgments

Chuck Bowden: 32, 84, 131, 197 (adapted from photographs from the following sources: 32, Nancy Crampton, courtesy Harper & Row Publishers, Inc.; 84, courtesy Viking Penguin, Inc.; 131, Rollie McKenna, courtesy Holt, Rinehart & Winston; 197, Rick Der, HBJ PHOTO); Sharon Harker: 63, 107, 165, 198–199 top, 208–209 top, 210 top, 211, 253, 272–273 top, 314; Susan Jaekel: 62, 83, 129, 153, 207; Jack Wallen: 31, 183, 237, 271, 318–320.

Cover: Tom Leonard.

Unit Openers: Willi Baum.

Contents

1 Tell Me Something Very Silly *11*

Dilly Dilly Piccalilli   A rhyme by Clyde Watson   *12*

Who Ever Sausage a Thing?   A rhyme   *13*

Pierre: A Cautionary Tale in Five Chapters and a Prologue
A story by Maurice Sendak   *14*

About MAURICE SENDAK   *32*

What Can They Be?
Riddles from Russia retold by Mirra Ginsburg   *33*

Oh, A-Hunting We Will Go   From an old song
with new verses by John Langstaff and friends   *34*

Solomon Grundy
A Mother Goose rhyme retold by Frederick Winsor   *38*

CONNECTIONS: **Riding on Two Wheels** (Social Studies)   *40*

"Fire! Fire!"   A rhyme   *48*

The Garden   A story by Arnold Lobel   *50*

BOOKSHELF   *63*

2 Something Is There *65*

Teeny-Tiny   An English folk tale retold by Joseph Jacobs   *66*

Something Is There   A poem by Lilian Moore   *71*

Grandfather's Story

From a story by Else Holmelund Minarik *72*

About ELSE HOLMELUND MINARIK *84*

A Ghost Story A Japanese rhyme *85*

CONNECTIONS: **Shadows** (Science) *86*

Sebastian and the Monster

From a story in pictures by Fernando Krahn *90*

We Three A poem by Lilian Moore *106*

BOOKSHELF *107*

3 I Can Do It! *109*

At the Top of My Voice A poem by Felice Holman *110*

Max A story by Rachel Isadora *112*

Walk Tall in the World A poem by Lucille Clifton *130*

About LUCILLE CLIFTON *131*

The Ant and the Dove

An Aesop fable retold by Anne Terry White *132*

Mary Jo's Grandfather From a story by Janice May Udry *136*

CONNECTIONS: **Safety Bear** (Health) *154*

Snowflakes drift A poem by Kazue Mizumura *160*

Soft Grass A poem *162*

Rope Rhyme A poem by Eloise Greenfield *164*

BOOKSHELF *165*

4 Animals All Around *167*

Can You Guess?

    Riddles in rhyme by Beatrice Schenk de Regniers *168*

Caballito   A Mexican rhyme *170*

Rrra-ah   From a story by Eros Keith *172*

You Can't Make a Turtle Come Out

    From a song by Malvina Reynolds *184*

<u>CONNECTIONS</u>: **Remarkable Reptiles** (Science) *186*

Three Little Animals   Poems by Ernesto Galarza *194*

About ERNESTO GALARZA *197*

LEARN ABOUT LIBRARIES: Animals in the Library *198*

Dinosaur Time   From a story by Peggy Parish *200*

LEARN ABOUT STORIES: "How" and "Why" Stories *208*

BOOKSHELF *211*

5 Long, Long Ago *213*

Heart of the Woods   A poem by Wesley Curtright *214*

The Magic Porridge Pot

    A German folk tale retold by Paul Galdone *216*

Some One   A poem by Walter de la Mare *228*

The Trolls and the Pussy Cat   Adapted from

    a Norwegian folk tale told by George Jonsen *230*

Socks for Supper   A story by Jack Kent *238*

Alarm Clock   A poem by Eve Merriam *252*

BOOKSHELF *253*

6 We Could Be Friends 255

We Could Be Friends A poem by Myra Cohn Livingston *256*

The Traveling Musicians A play based on
a German folk tale collected by the Brothers Grimm *258*

LEARN ABOUT STORIES: **Follow the Road to Bremen** *272*

The Elves and the Shoemaker Adapted from the
German folk tale collected by the Brothers Grimm *274*

CONNECTIONS: **A Sneaker Factory** (Social Studies) *284*

Split Pea Soup A story by James Marshall *292*

Grandfather From a poem by Shirley Crawford *299*

Crystal Is the New Girl From a story by Shirley Gordon *300*

Spinning Song A poem by Zilpha Keatley Snyder *312*

BOOKSHELF *314*

KEY WORDS *315*

SOUNDS AND LETTERS *318*

1 Tell Me Something Very Silly

Dilly Dilly Piccalilli

A rhyme by Clyde Watson

Dilly Dilly Piccalilli
Tell me something very silly:
There was a chap his name was Bert
He ate the buttons off his shirt.

Who Ever Sausage a Thing?

A rhyme

One day a girl went walking
And went into a store;
She bought a pound of sausages
And laid them on the floor.

The girl began to whistle
A merry little tune—
And all the little sausages
Danced around the room!

Pictures by Dora Leder

PIERRE

a cautionary tale
IN
FIVE CHAPTERS
AND A
PROLOGUE

Story and pictures
by Maurice Sendak

Prologue

*There once was a boy
named Pierre
who only would say,*
"I don't care!"
*Read his story,
my friend,
for you'll find
at the end
that a suitable
moral lies there.*

Chapter 1

One day
his mother said
when Pierre
climbed out of bed,
"Good morning,
darling boy,
you are
my only joy."
Pierre said,
"I don't care!"

"What would you
like to eat?"
"I don't care!"
"Some lovely
cream of wheat?"
"I don't care!"
"Don't sit backwards
on your chair."
"I don't care!"
"Or pour syrup
on your hair."
"I don't care!"

16

"You are acting
like a clown."
"I don't care!"
"And we have
to go to town."
"I don't care!"
"Don't you want
to come, my dear?"
"I don't care!"
"Would you rather
stay right here?"
"I don't care!"

So his mother
left him there.

Chapter 2

His father said,
"Get off your head
or I will march you
up to bed!"
Pierre said,
"I don't care!"
"I would think
that you could see—"
"I don't care!"
"Your head is where
your feet should be!"
"I don't care!"

"If you keep standing
upside down—"
"I don't care!"
"We'll never ever
get to town."
"I don't care!"
"If only you would
say I CARE."
"I don't care!"
"I'd let you fold
the folding chair."
"I don't care!"

So his parents
left him there.
They didn't take him
anywhere.

Chapter 3

Now, as the night
began to fall
a hungry lion
paid a call.
He looked Pierre
right in the eye
and asked him
if he'd like to die.
Pierre said,
"I don't care!"

"I can eat you,
don't you see?"
"I don't care!"
"And you will be
inside of me."
"I don't care!"
"Then you'll never
have to bother—"
"I don't care!"
"With a mother
and a father."
"I don't care!"

"Is that all
you have to say?"
"I don't care!"
"Then I'll eat you,
if I may."
"I don't care!"

So the lion
ate Pierre.

Chapter 4

Arriving home
at six o'clock,
his parents had
a dreadful shock!
They found the lion
sick in bed
and cried,
"Pierre is surely dead!"

They pulled the lion
by the hair.
They hit him
with the folding chair.
His mother asked,
"Where is Pierre?"
The lion answered,
"I don't care!"
His father said,
"Pierre's in there!"

Chapter 5

They rushed the lion
into town.
The doctor shook him
up and down.
And when the lion
gave a roar—
Pierre fell out
upon the floor.
He rubbed his eyes
and scratched his head
and laughed
because he wasn't dead.

His mother cried
and held him tight.
His father asked,
"Are you all right?"
Pierre said,
"I am feeling fine,
please take me home,
it's half past nine."
The lion said,
"If you would care
to climb on me,
I'll take you there."
Then everyone
looked at Pierre
who shouted,
"Yes, indeed I care!!"

The lion took them
home to rest
and stayed on
as a weekend guest.

The moral of Pierre
is: CARE!

Questions

1. Tell three things Pierre did to show he did not care.

2. What changed Pierre's mind about not caring?

3. When Pierre's father looked at the lion, he said, "Pierre's in there." How did he know?

4. A lion "paid a call." What does *paid a call* mean?

5. Pierre's parents were "shocked." What does *shocked* mean?

6. The story has a "moral." What does *moral* mean?

    guest   surprise   lesson

Activity Write About Feelings

Pierre, you used to say, "I don't care." Why did you say that? Help Pierre answer. Write what he might say.

About MAURICE SENDAK

Did anyone ever tell stories to you when you were sick? As a boy, Maurice Sendak was sick for a very long time. During that time, his father made up stories for him and his brother and sister.

When he was nine, Maurice Sendak began writing his own stories. He often hand-lettered the stories and drew pictures to go with them. When he was older, he spent many hours at his window drawing the children playing outside. One of them was a girl named Rosie.

Many years later, Maurice Sendak wrote a book about Rosie called *The Sign on Rosie's Door.* He has written and illustrated many other stories as well that people of all ages enjoy.

More Books by Maurice Sendak

Higglety Pigglety Pop! or There Must Be More to Life
Where the Wild Things Are
The Nutshell Library
Outside Over There

What Can They Be?

Two riddles from Russia retold by Mirra Ginsburg

He wears a wooden shirt,
And his nose is dark.
Wherever he goes,
He leaves a mark.

(A pencil.)

When they are empty, they stand,
When they are full, they walk.

(Shoes.)

Oh, A-Hunting We Will Go

An old song with new verses by John Langstaff and friends

Oh, a-hunting we will go,
A-hunting we will go,
We'll catch a fox
And put it in a box,
And then we'll let it go!

Pictures by Marie-Louise Gay

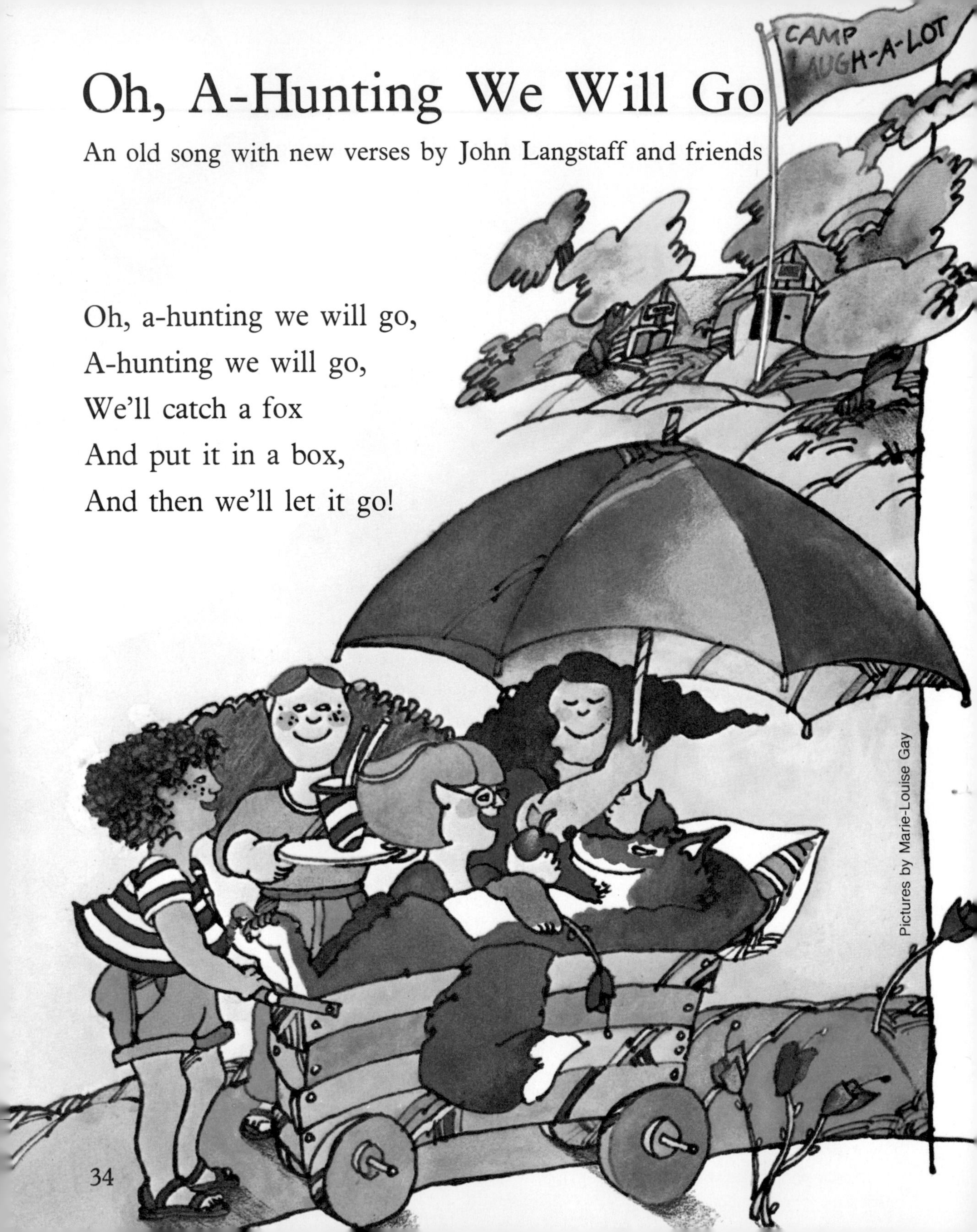

Oh, a-hunting we will go,
A-hunting we will go,
We'll catch a goat
And put it in a boat,
And then we'll let it go!

Oh, a-hunting we will go,
A-hunting we will go,
We'll catch a skunk
And put it in a bunk,
And then we'll let it go!

Oh, a-hunting we will go,
A-hunting we will go,
We'll catch a brontosaurus
And put it in a chorus,
And then we'll let it go!

Solomon Grundy

A Mother Goose rhyme retold by Frederick Winsor

Solomon Grundy
Walked on Monday
Rode on Tuesday
Motored Wednesday
Planed on Thursday
Rocketed Friday
Spaceship Saturday
Time Machine Sunday
Where is the end for
Solomon Grundy?

38

Picture by Jim M'Guiness

Riding on Two Wheels

Long ago, there were no cars or buses. So people got from place to place in other ways. Some people used a two-wheeled machine called a *bicycle*.

The first bicycles looked very different from bicycles today. Many of the early bicycles were hard to ride.

Pictures by Gwen Connelly

hobbyhorse

At first, people rode a bicycle called a
hobbyhorse. It had no pedals. Riders had to
sit on a hard seat. Then they would put
their feet on the ground and push!

Many years later, someone made a
bicycle with pedals. The wheels were made
of wood. So the ride was very bumpy!
People called this bicycle the *bone-shaker*.

bone-shaker

A funny-looking bicycle was the *ordinary*. It had a very big front wheel. It had a very small back wheel. It was hard to get on this high-wheeler. The ordinary was so tall that people had to stand on something to reach the seat. Then, sitting up so high made it easy to fall off! When riders fell off, they pushed their bicycles until they found something to stand on again. Then they could get back on and ride.

ordinary

safety

The ordinary was hard to use. So
someone thought of a new kind of bicycle.
It was called the *safety*. The safety had two
wheels of the same size. This made it easier
and safer to ride than bicycles before it.
The safety was so much fun to ride that
people started bicycle-riding clubs. People
in the clubs would go on long rides
together.

tandem

The *tandem* was a bicycle that was built for two people. This bicycle had two seats and two handlebars. One rider sat behind the other. Both riders had their own set of pedals.

The tandem was first made many years ago, but it is still used today.

More people ride bicycles today than ever before. People ride bicycles for fun and for exercise. Boys and girls often ride bicycles to school or to do small jobs. Some grown-ups ride bicycles to and from work.

There is a special bicycle for each of these uses.

Bicycles have changed many times since they were first used. However, people still like to ride them just the same. In our country, about one out of every three people rides a bicycle today.

BIKE PATH

Questions

1. What does the word *bicycle* mean?

   two   three   four
   wheels   wheels   wheels

2. Which bicycle had no pedals?

3. Why was it so hard to get on the ordinary bicycle?

4. Which bicycle was made for two people?

5. How are a bicycle and a car alike? How are they different?

Activity   Practice Hand Signals

Bicycle riders use hand signals to show that they will turn or stop. Practice the hand signals in the picture. Then copy the hand signals on another piece of paper and write a sentence that tells how each is used.

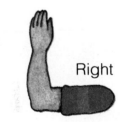
Right

Left

Stop

"Fire! Fire!"

A rhyme

"Fire! Fire!"
Cried Mrs. McGuire.
"Where! Where!"
Cried Mrs. Blair.
"All over town!"
Cried Mrs. Brown.
"Get some water!"
Cried Mrs. Carter.
"We'd better jump!"
Cried Mrs. Gump.
"That would be silly!"
Cried Mrs. Brunelli.
"It looks too risky!"
Cried Mrs. Matruski.
"What'll we do?"
Cried Mrs. LaRue.
"Turn in an alarm!"
Cried Mrs. Storm.
"Save us! Save us!"
Cried Mrs. Davis.

The fire department got the call
And the firemen saved them, one and all.

Picture by Raphael & Bolognese

49

The Garden

Story and pictures by Arnold Lobel

Frog was in his garden.

Toad came walking by.

"What a fine garden
you have, Frog," he said.

"Yes," said Frog. "It is very nice,
but it was hard work."

"I wish I had a garden," said Toad.

"Here are some flower seeds.
Plant them in the ground," said Frog,
"and soon you will have a garden."

"How soon?" asked Toad.

"Quite soon," said Frog.

Toad ran home.

He planted the flower seeds.

"Now, seeds," said Toad,
"start growing."

Toad walked up and down
a few times.

The seeds did not start to grow.

Toad put his head
close to the ground
and said loudly, "Now, seeds,
start growing!"

Toad looked at the ground again.
The seeds did not start to grow.

Toad put his head
very close to the ground and shouted,
"NOW, SEEDS, START GROWING!"
Frog came running up the path.
"What is all this noise?" he asked.
"My seeds will not grow," said Toad.
"You are shouting too much,"
said Frog. "These poor seeds
are afraid to grow."
"My seeds are afraid to grow?"
asked Toad.

"Of course," said Frog.

"Leave them alone for a few days.

Let the sun shine on them,

let the rain fall on them.

Soon your seeds will start to grow."

That night Toad looked out
of his window.

"Drat!" said Toad. "My seeds
have not started to grow.
They must be afraid of the dark."

Toad went out to his garden
with some candles.

"I will read the seeds a story,"
said Toad. "Then they will not
be afraid."

Toad read a long story
to his seeds.

All the next day
Toad sang songs
to his seeds.

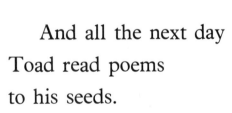

And all the next day
Toad read poems
to his seeds.

And all the next day
Toad played music
for his seeds.

Toad looked at the ground.
The seeds still did not
start to grow.
"What shall I do?"
cried Toad. "These must be
the most frightened seeds
in the whole world!"

Then Toad felt very tired,
and he fell asleep.

"Toad, Toad, wake up," said Frog.
"Look at your garden!"

Toad looked at his garden.
Little green plants were coming up
out of the ground.

"At last," shouted Toad,
"my seeds have stopped
being afraid to grow!"

"And now you will have
a nice garden too," said Frog.

"Yes," said Toad,
"but you were right, Frog.
It was very hard work."

Questions

1. Frog told Toad how to make seeds grow. Tell two things Frog said.

2. Toad did funny things to make his seeds grow. Tell what Toad did.

3. How would *you* make seeds grow?

4. Frog said Toad's seeds would come up ''quite soon.'' What did ''quite soon'' mean to Toad?

5. What did Frog mean by ''quite soon''?

Activity   **Draw a Surprise**

We are little green plants in Toad's garden. We are going to give Toad and Frog a very big surprise. What will the surprise be? We want it to be a happy surprise. When Toad and Frog come to see us tomorrow, what will they find? Draw our surprise. Write what it is under your drawing.

BOOKSHELF

A Great Big Ugly Man Came Up and Tied His Horse to Me: A Book of Nonsense Verse. Pictures by Wallace Tripp. Little, Brown, 1973. This book has many silly rhymes, old and new. The pictures are as funny as the rhymes.

Riddle Rat by Donald Hall. Frederick Warne, 1977. Riddle Rat guesses the answers to all Aunt Agatha's riddles. Soon he is making up his own riddles.

Lambs for Dinner by Betsy Maestro. Crown, 1978. A hungry wolf invites a family of lambs to dinner. The menu is a surprise.

Bunny Rabbit Rebus by David Adler. T. Y. Crowell, 1983. In this funny rebus story, pictures take the place of soundalike words. For example, a picture of a *bee* takes the place of the word *be.*

Curious George by H. A. Rey. Houghton Mifflin, 1941. (Spanish edition: **Jorge el curioso,** Houghton Mifflin, 1961) A curious little African monkey named George gets into mischief time after time.

2 Something Is There

Teeny-Tiny

An English folk tale
retold by Joseph Jacobs
Pictures by Stephen Osborn

Once upon a time
there was a teeny-tiny woman
who lived in a teeny-tiny house
in a teeny-tiny town.

Now one day this teeny-tiny woman
put on her teeny-tiny bonnet
and went out of her teeny-tiny house
to take a teeny-tiny walk.

And when this teeny-tiny woman
had gone a teeny-tiny way,
she came to a teeny-tiny gate.
So the teeny-tiny woman
opened the teeny-tiny gate
and went into a teeny-tiny churchyard.

And when this teeny-tiny woman
had got into the teeny-tiny churchyard,
she saw a teeny-tiny bone.
The teeny-tiny woman
said to her teeny-tiny self,
"This teeny-tiny bone
will make me some teeny-tiny soup
for my teeny-tiny supper."

So the teeny-tiny woman
put the teeny-tiny bone
into her teeny-tiny pocket
and went home to her teeny-tiny house.

Now when the teeny-tiny woman
got home to her teeny-tiny house,
she was a teeny-tiny bit tired.
So she went up her teeny-tiny stairs
to her teeny-tiny bed
and put the teeny-tiny bone
into a teeny-tiny cupboard.

And when this teeny-tiny woman
had been asleep a teeny-tiny time,
she was awakened by a teeny-tiny voice
from the teeny-tiny cupboard,
that said,

"Give me my bone!"

And this teeny-tiny woman
was a teeny-tiny bit frightened.
So she hid her teeny-tiny head
under the teeny-tiny covers
and went to sleep again.

And when she had been asleep again
a teeny-tiny time,
the teeny-tiny voice again
cried out from the teeny-tiny cupboard
a teeny-tiny louder,

This made the teeny-tiny woman
a teeny-tiny bit more frightened.
So she hid her teeny-tiny head
a teeny-tiny farther
under the teeny-tiny covers.

And when the teeny-tiny woman
had been asleep again
a teeny-tiny time,
the teeny-tiny voice
from the teeny-tiny cupboard
said again a teeny-tiny louder,

"Give me my bone!"

And this teeny-tiny woman
was a teeny-tiny bit more frightened.
But she put her teeny-tiny head
out of the teeny-tiny covers
and said in her loudest teeny-tiny voice,

TAKE IT!

Something Is There

A poem by Lilian Moore

Something is there
there on the stair
coming down
coming down
stepping with care.
Coming down
coming down
slinkety-sly.

Something is coming and wants to get by.

Grandfather's Story

From the story *Little Bear's Visit* by Else Holmelund Minarik

Pictures by Maurice Sendak

"Grandfather," asked Little Bear,
"how about a goblin story?"

"Yes, if you will hold my paw,"
said Grandfather.

"I will not be scared," said Little Bear.

"No," said Grandfather Bear.
"But I may be scared."

"Oh, Grandfather! Begin the story."

So Grandfather began.

One day a little goblin
went by an old cave.
It was old,
it was cold,
it was dark.

And something inside it went bump.

What was that?

BUMP!

"Hoo—ooh——" cried the goblin.

He got so scared that he jumped
right out of his shoes.
Then he began to run.

Pit–pat–pit–pat–pit–pat——

What was that?

SOMETHING was running after him.

Oh, my goodness, what could it be?

The goblin was too scared to look back.

He ran faster than ever.

But so did the SOMETHING that went

pit–pat–pit–pat–pit–pat——

The goblin saw a hole in a tree.
He jumped inside to hide.
The pit–pat–pit–pat came closer,
closer—CLOSER—till it stopped,
right by the hole in the tree!

Then all was quiet.
Nothing happened.
Nothing.

The little goblin wanted to peek out.
It was so quiet.
Should he peek out?
Yes, he would. He WOULD peek out!
And he did.

"Eeeeeh——!" cried the goblin.

Do you know what he saw?

He saw—his SHOES!
His own little shoes
——and nothing more.
"Goodness," said the goblin,
hopping out of the tree.

"That old bump in the cave
made me jump right out of my shoes.
But they came running after me,
didn't they!
And here they are!"

He picked up his shoes,
hugged them,
and put them back on.

"Good little shoes," said the goblin.
"You didn't want to stay behind,
did you!" He laughed.
"Who cares about an old bump,
anyway," he said.
So he snapped his fingers,
and skipped away——

"——just like that!" said Grandfather.

"I can't jump out of my shoes,"
said Little Bear,
"because I don't have any."
He chuckled. "That's how I like it."

Questions

1. Why did Little Bear hold Grandfather's paw?

2. What did the goblin do when he heard the BUMP?

3. Why did the goblin hug his shoes?

4. Why do you think Grandfather told this story?
   a. to scare Little Bear
   b. to make Little Bear chuckle
   c. to put Little Bear to sleep

5. What do you think Little Bear will do when he hears something go BUMP?

Activity   Draw and Write What Happens

It is night. You are walking down the street. You hear THUMP, THUMP behind you. Draw a picture to show what made the THUMP, THUMP. Write a sentence to tell what you would do.

About ELSE HOLMELUND MINARIK

A little girl wanted to read when she was still very young. So her mother wrote books for her. A class of first graders did not have books to read during the summer. So their teacher wrote some stories for them.

The mother and teacher who wrote those books is Else Holmelund Minarik. The books she wrote are called the *Little Bear* books, and you can still enjoy her stories about Little Bear, his family, and his friends.

More Books by Else Holmelund Minarik

Little Bear
Little Bear's Friend
Father Bear Comes Home
A Kiss for Little Bear
Little Bear's Visit
No Fighting, No Biting
Cat and Dog
The Little Giant Girl and the Elf Boy

A Ghost Story

A Japanese rhyme

"Hello, you, are you a ghost,
Hiding there behind that post?"

"No, I'm just an old dead tree—
You needn't be afraid of me."

Picture by Kinuko Craft

CONNECTIONS

Shadows

Look around you. Shadows are everywhere. They can be big or small, long or short, fat or thin. Shadows can dance about or sit very still. Sometimes shadows can be funny, sometimes they can be scary.

Who has not been frightened by a shadow? Shadows can look like a ghost on a tree, a monster on a fence, or a creature on a house.

Pictures by Larry Frederick

Shadows are made with light. The light may come from something as large as the sun or as small as a candle.

Light cannot pass through many things. It cannot pass through a tree, for example. The light from the sun hits the tree. The light goes around the tree, but it cannot pass through the tree. In the place where the light is blocked, a shadow is formed.

When the light changes its place, the shape of the shadow changes. The shadow will be short and fat when the light is high above the tree. The shadow will be long and thin when the light is low in the sky.

a hawk crying

a duck
walking

Shadows can be useful and fun. Some storytellers use shadows to tell stories. The children in the picture are telling a shadow story about an eagle, a duck, and a hawk. To make the shadow puppets, the three storytellers block the light with their hands. Their hands make shadows on the wall. As the storytellers move their hands slowly, the shadow puppets seem to move and talk.

an eagle flying

Questions

1. How is a shadow formed?

2. Which things below can make light?
   sun   lamp   wall   fire

3. Which things made each shadow?

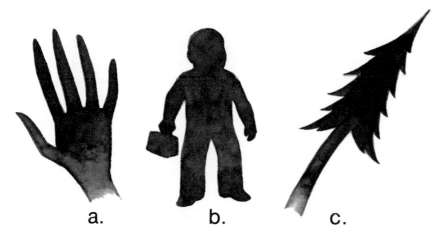

a.   b.   c.

4. Tell about the sun in each picture
   above. Is it high or low in the sky?

Activity   **Tell a Shadow Story**

Tell a story using shadow puppets.
You may want to use the duck, rabbit,
dog, and turkey shown in the pictures.
Try other shadow puppets, too.

Write your story on a piece of paper.

duck   rabbit

dog

turkey

Sebastian and the Monster

A picture story by Fernando Krahn

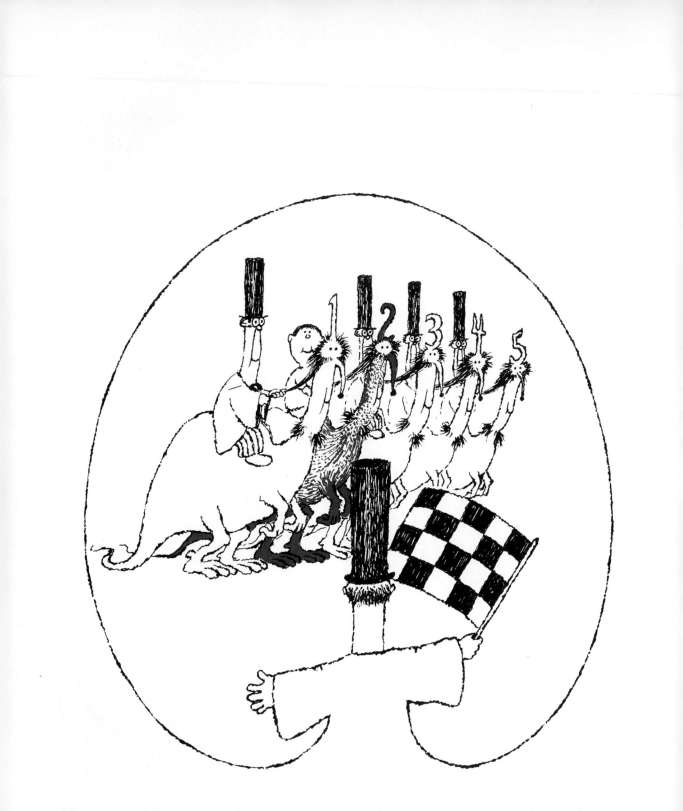

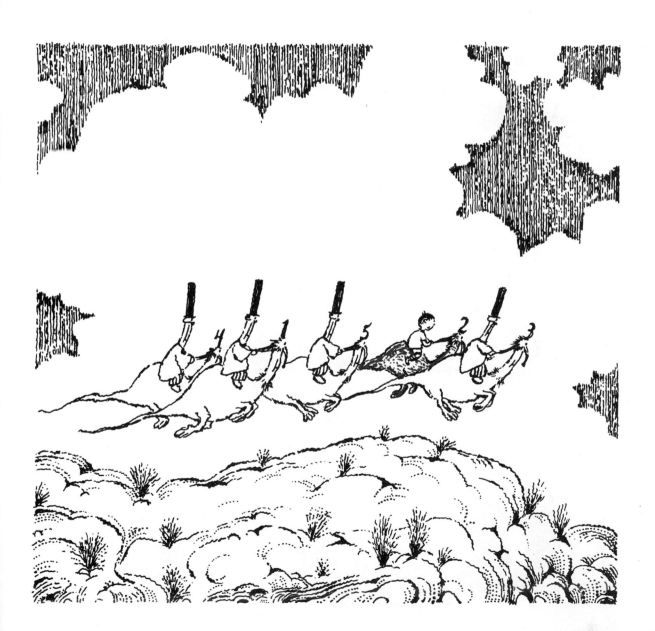

We Three

A poem by Lilian Moore

We three
went out on Halloween,
A Pirate
An Ape
A Witch between.

We went from door to door.

By the light
of the moon
these shadows were seen
A Pirate
An Ape
A Witch between
and—

Say, how did we get to be FOUR?

Picture by Tom Durfee

BOOKSHELF

You're the Scaredy Cat by Mercer Mayer. Parents' Magazine Press, 1974. An older brother tells a scary story to frighten his younger brother. Both brothers are scared, but only one is the scaredy cat.

Moon Bear by Frank Asch. Charles Scribner's Sons, 1978. Bear sees the moon growing smaller every night. Is the moon going to disappear? Whom can he tell?

The King's Monster by Carolyn Haywood. William Morrow, 1980. Though the princess Gabriella is old enough to be married, the monster in her father's dungeon frightens away any young men.

America's Very Own Monsters by Daniel Cohen. Dodd, Mead, 1982. These are stories of Bigfoot and other monsterlike creatures to read and decide if you believe in monsters or not.

Georgie by Robert Bright. Doubleday, 1959. (Spanish edition: **Jorgito.** Doubleday, 1977) A ghost that's not at all scary, but really very friendly.

108

3 I Can Do It!

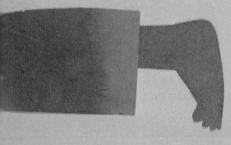

At the Top of My Voice

A poem by Felice Holman

When I stamp
The ground thunders,
When I shout
The world rings,
When I sing
The air wonders
How I do such things.

Picture by Ronni Shepherd

111

MAX

Story and pictures by Rachel Isadora

Max is a great baseball player.
He can run fast, jump high, and hardly
ever misses a ball. Every Saturday he
plays with his team in the park.

On Saturday mornings he walks with
his sister Lisa to her dancing school.
The school is on the way to the park.

One Saturday when they reach the school,
Max still has lots of time before
the game is to start. Lisa asks him
if he wants to come inside for a while.

Max doesn't really want to, but he says
O.K. Soon the class begins. He gets
a chair and sits near the door to watch.

The teacher invites Max
to join the class, but he must
take off his sneakers first.

He stretches at the *barre*.   He tries to do the split.

And the *pas de chat*. He is having fun.

119

Just as the class lines up to do leaps
across the floor, Lisa points to the clock.
It is time for Max to leave.

Max doesn't want to miss the leaps.
He waits and takes his turn.

Then he must go.
He leaps all the way to the park.

He is late.

Everybody is waiting for him.

He goes up to bat.

Strike one!

He tries again.

Strike two!

And then . . .

A home run!

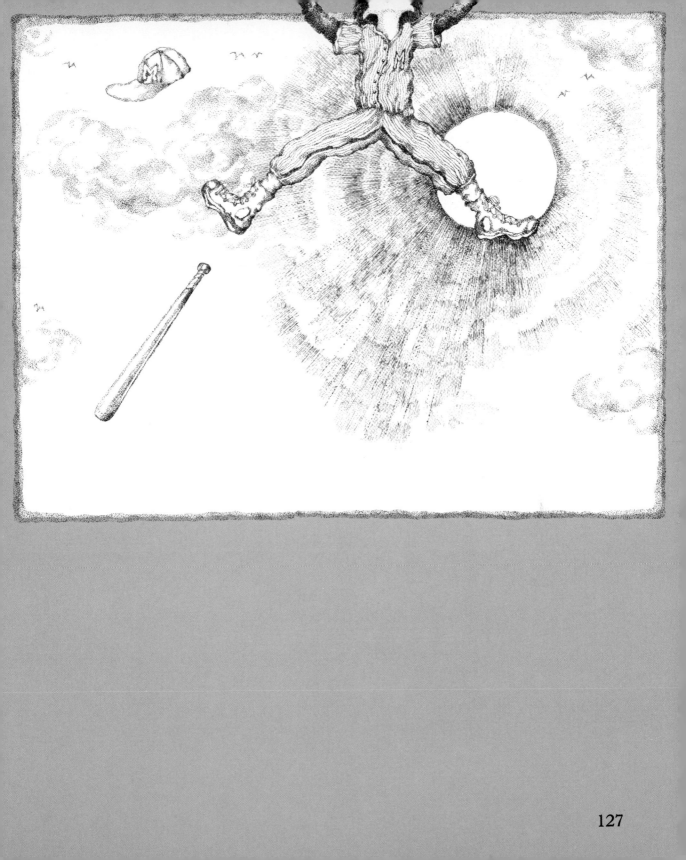

Now Max has a new way to warm up
for the game on Saturdays.
He goes to dancing class.

Questions

1. What did Max find out about dancing?

2. What exciting thing did Max do in the baseball game?

3. Tell what Max does on Saturdays now.

4. Someone says, "Baseball players don't dance." What does Max say?

5. A riddle for you: How is a dancer like a baseball player?
   a. Both keep score.
   b. Both must warm up.
   c. Both tell stories.

6. Which three words in the story tell how dancers move?

Activity   Tell About Learning Something New

Max learned to do something new. He learned to dance. What new thing would you like to learn to do? Tell or write how you would try to learn to do it. Tell or write who might teach you.

Walk Tall in the World

A poem by Lucille Clifton

"Walk tall in the world,"
says Mama
to Everett Anderson.
"The year is new and
so are the days,
walk tall in the world,"
she says.

Picture by Carol Newsom

About LUCILLE CLIFTON

The mother of six children, Lucille Clifton writes poems and stories about children. She writes of what they like to do and how they feel: happy, sad, angry, proud.

Several of Lucille Clifton's books are about a boy named Everett Anderson. If you read them, you may discover you've done some of the things Everett Anderson has done. Maybe you and Everett Anderson sometimes feel the same way, too.

More Books by Lucille Clifton

Everett Anderson's Year
Everett Anderson's Friend
Everett Anderson's 1-2-3
Everett Anderson's Nine Month Long
My Brother Fine with Me
The Boy Who Didn't Believe in Spring
The Lucky Stone
My Friend Jacob

The Ant and the Dove

An Aesop fable retold by Anne Terry White

Pictures by Christa Kieffer

A thirsty Ant was climbing down
a blade of grass that grew beside a
spring. She was trying to reach
the water so she could take a drink.
Unluckily she slipped and fell into
the spring.

Now a Dove was sitting on a branch over the water. She saw the Ant fall in and was filled with pity. Quick as a wink she pulled off a leaf and let it fall into the spring.

The little raft settled down on the water right beside the drowning Ant. The Ant climbed on the leaf and was soon safe on shore again.

But what did she see? Hidden behind
a bush, a hunter was spreading his net.
He was going to catch the Dove!

"No!" the grateful Ant said.
"You shall not take the bird that saved
my life!" And with all her might she bit
the hunter on his bare foot.

With a cry the hunter dropped his net,
and the Dove flew away to the wood.

One good turn deserves another.

Mary Jo's Grandmother

Adapted from the story by Janice May Udry

Pictures by Charles Robinson

Mary Jo's grandmother was quite old. She lived alone in a little house in the country.

Whenever Mary Jo's mother or father told Grandmother that she should move into town, Grandmother always said, "I've lived in this house almost all my life. I'm too old to move now. I'm happy here."

The family drove out to visit Grandmother often. In the spring they helped her plant a vegetable garden and flowers. Mary Jo played with the baby chicks and fed the hens.

In the summer Mary Jo and her brother Jeff waded in the creek. They picked blackberries.

Mary Jo's father always told Grandmother, "You still make the best berry pie in the world."

And Mary Jo's grandmother always laughed and said, "You just say that because it's true."

But after the leaves began to fall from the trees and the days grew colder, Mary Jo's mother and father began to worry.

"You haven't even got a telephone. You shouldn't be living all alone way out here," said Mary Jo's mother. "Why, your nearest neighbor is out beyond the main road."

Grandmother smiled. "Now don't you worry about me. I'm as snug as can be here. Don't you fret about me."

Every year the family had Christmas dinner at Grandmother's. This year, for the first time, Mary Jo was staying on at Grandmother's by herself. After dinner she and Grandmother waved good-bye to everybody from the porch. It was very quiet. Grandmother looked out over the bare trees at the sky. "Snow tonight," she said.

Just before she fell asleep, Mary Jo saw great flakes of snow, like feathers, falling outside the window.

Even though Mary Jo woke early next morning, she could already hear Grandmother in the kitchen.

"Beautiful snow, beautiful snow," sang Mary Jo when she looked out the window.

"This is the most snow I ever saw here this early in the winter," said Grandmother, putting biscuits into the oven. "Here, Mary Jo, take these bread crumbs out to the birds. I'm going to get some jam from the back pantry."

Mary Jo had to sweep the snow ahead of herself so she could walk out on the porch. She swept one corner of the porch. Then she put out the crumbs. Before she was back inside the door, hungry birds were there to eat.

Grandmother had not come back from the pantry yet. From the open pantry door, Mary Jo heard a moan. Grandmother called, "Mary Jo!"

"What happened?" said Mary Jo running to the door. She looked down. Her grandmother was lying on the pantry floor. She had fallen down the steps.

"I can't get up," moaned Grandmother.

"I'm coming! I'll help you," said Mary Jo.

"Take the biscuits out of the oven first," said Grandmother.

Mary Jo hurried to the oven, opened the door, and lifted the biscuits out. Then she hurried to the pantry. But when Mary Jo knelt beside her grandmother and tried to lift her, Grandmother cried out with pain.

"No, Mary Jo, don't try to lift me. My leg hurts too much to move it," she said. "Now I'm in a fine fix!"

"Don't worry, Grandmother," said Mary Jo. She ran into the bedroom and got blankets to wrap around her grandmother. She carefully put a pillow under her head.

"Thank goodness you are here, Mary Jo," Grandmother said. "Just let me rest while I think of what to do. I'll be all right. You go and have some breakfast while the biscuits are hot."

Mary Jo poured some coffee for her grandmother. Then, while she ate a biscuit, she looked out the window at the falling snow. I don't even have my boots here, she thought.

Mary Jo knew that she must go for help. On a day like this, no one would be passing by on the little road where her grandmother lived. She would have to walk to the main road.

"I'm going up to the main road for help," said Mary Jo.

"In all this snow?" said Grandmother.

"I can do it," said Mary Jo.

Grandmother sighed. "I guess I'll have to let you go, Mary Jo," she said. "Wrap up good and warm."

"Yes, Grandmother," said Mary Jo. "You rest and don't worry."

"I'll be all right. I'm a tough old bird," said Grandmother. Then she leaned her head back and closed her eyes.

Mary Jo found a pair of boots in a
closet. She made them fit by stuffing the
toes full of newspaper. She put on two
sweaters, a coat, and an old stocking cap.
Then she hurried out into the snow.

The snow had stopped falling, but icy
wind blew into her face. Mary Jo walked
as fast as she could down the long drive.

It took her twice as long as it usually
did just to reach the old mailbox. The
snow in the road was untouched. No truck
or car had been along.

Mary Jo walked on toward the main
road, lifting her feet high at each step in
the old heavy boots. She had never felt so
much alone.

When she finally reached the main
highway, Mary Jo could see that no cars
had been along there, either. The snow was
too deep. Mary Jo's legs had never felt so
tired.

Then up the road she saw a black speck
moving slowly closer. She stared at it.
Then she waved. "It's the snowplow!" she
cried out loud.

It seemed to take forever for the snowplow to reach Mary Jo. She jumped up and down to keep warm, even though her legs were aching.

The driver stopped and leaned over. "What are you doing out here, little girl?"

Mary Jo explained to him what had happened. "Can you call my father in town? His name is William Wood."

"Sure!" said the man. "Here, climb up. We'll clear the road down to your grandmother's house. We'll let you off there. Then I'll go on to the next house and phone your father."

When Mary Jo got off at her grandmother's drive, she waved good-bye and walked back up to the house.

Grandmother's eyes were open and she smiled. "How did you get back so fast, child?"

Mary Jo told her about the snowplow. "Mother and Dad will be here in a little while," she said. "All our worries are over now, Grandmother. I'll go heat some soup."

"That sounds good," said Grandmother. "I'm feeling better already. Thank goodness you were here, Mary Jo."

Questions

1. How did Mary Jo show she was brave?

2. How did Grandmother show she was brave?

3. You are the snowplow driver. What else could you have done to help Mary Jo and her grandmother?

4. "I'm as snug as can be," Grandmother said. What does "snug" mean?

   funny   hurried   cozy

5. "Don't fret about me," said Mary Jo's grandmother. What does "fret" mean?

   smile   worry   think

6. What do you think happened after the story ended?

Activity   Write a Safety List

Mary Jo's grandmother still wants to live in the country. Mary Jo is making a list of things that Grandmother can do to be safe in the country. Add three more things to Mary Jo's list.

To Be Safe
1. Put a light in the pantry.
2.
3.
4.

Safety Bear

My name is Safety Bear. My job is to check this house to see if the family follows safety rules. A safe home can keep people from getting hurt.

Take a close look at this house. No shoes or toys are on the stairs. Playing on the stairs or leaving things on them could cause someone to fall.

Pictures by Janet Lasalle

Look at this picture. It shows how to safely carry something sharp. Always hold the sharp part toward the floor. Walk, never run, when holding something sharp. Sharp things must be kept away from small children.

Matches, medicines, and cleaners are locked away in this house. Babies are safe from them. These are not playthings.

The children in this house cannot reach the high shelves in the kitchen. They ask a grown-up to reach for the things they want. Then the children will not fall and get hurt.

When something spills, the children clean up the spill well. Wet floors can cause someone to slip and fall.

This family has a plan if there is a fire. The family must get out of the house quickly. If the house is full of smoke, the people will crawl out. Clean air stays near the floor. The family will meet outside the house. No one will go back into the house until the fire is out.

Telephone numbers for the police, fire department, and ambulance are kept where they can be seen quickly.

The children who live here have bicycles. Only one person rides on a bicycle at a time. They ride close to the right-hand side of the road. They keep both hands on the handlebars. They never make their bicycles jump over steps or curbs. When crossing the street, they walk the bicycles across. Every time they ride, they follow good safety rules.

My safety check is done. This family will get my highest award: the Safety Bear Safety Seal.

Questions

1. Which one is being carried safely?

   a.   b.   c.

2. Which stairs are safe?

   a.   b.   c.

3. Which of these is safe to play with?

   a.   b.   c.

4. What can *you* do to make your home safe? List three things.

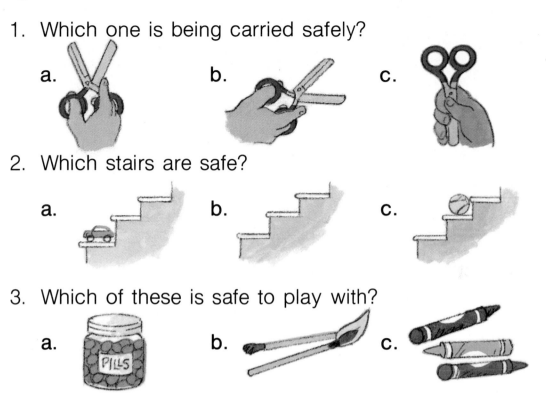

Activity   Make a Safety Poster

The children made a Safety Bear poster for their home. The poster reminds them of one of Safety Bear's safety rules. Make a Safety Bear poster for your home.

Snowflakes drift.
I taste winter
melting on my lips.

A poem by Kazue Mizumura

Soft Grass

A poem

The sidewalk is hard
Beneath my feet.
Hard, hot sidewalk,
Hard, hot street.

Stony sidewalk,
Stony yard,
Stony buildings,
Hot and hard.

But I go to the park
Along my street,
Where the grass is soft
Beneath my feet.

Picture by Carol Newsom

Off of the sidewalk,
Out of the sun,
Over the cool, soft grass
I run!

Rope Rhyme

A poem by Eloise Greenfield

Get set, ready now, jump right in
Bounce and kick and giggle and spin
Listen to the rope when it hits the ground
Listen to that clappedy-slappedy sound
Jump right up when it tells you to
Come back down, whatever you do
Count to a hundred, count by ten
Start to count all over again
That's what jumping is all about
Get set, ready now, jump right out!

Picture by Sharon Harker

BOOKSHELF

"I Can't," Said the Ant by Polly Cameron. Coward, McCann & Geoghegan, 1961. Miss Teapot falls and breaks her spout. An army of ants and spiders come to help her.

I Can Do It Myself by Lessie Jones Little and Eloise Greenfield. T. Y. Crowell, 1978. Donny wants to buy his mother a birthday present. He goes to the store with his wagon all by himself, but a big bulldog gets in his way going home.

Aesop's Fables by Aesop. Illustrated by Heidi Holder. Viking Press, 1981. A book of lesson-teaching stories worth remembering.

St. Patrick's Day in the Morning by Anne Eve Bunting. Houghton Mifflin, 1980. A small boy proves he is big enough and strong enough to walk in the holiday parade through his Irish hometown.

Amelia's Flying Machine by Barbara Shook Hazen. Doubleday, 1977. When Amelia Earhart was a little girl, she already wanted to fly and be free like the birds, so she built a flying machine in her back yard!

Animals
All Around

Can You Guess?

Riddles in rhyme by Beatrice Schenk de Regniers

It has two feet,
No hands, two wings.
It can fly
In the sky.

Sometimes it chirps.
Sometimes it sings
The sweetest song
You ever heard.
Can you guess?
It is a . . .

bird.

Six legs for walking.
Mouth for eating—not talking.
Does not make a sound.
Sleeps under the ground.
Likes picnics, but can't
Bring its own. It's an . . .

ant.

A short short tail.
A long long nose
It uses for
A water hose.

Two great big ears.
Four great big feet.
A tiny peanut
Is a treat.

Its name is El—
Oh, no! I can't!
Now *you* tell *me:*
An . . .

elephant.

169

Caballito

A Mexican rhyme

Caballito, caballito,
No me tumbes, no me tumbes;
a galope y a galope
recio, recio, recio.
¡Qué viva Antonio!

Little pony, little pony,
Do not throw me, do not throw me;
Galloping, galloping,
Watch us go!
Long live Antonio!

Picture by Raphael & Bolognese

Rrra-ah

From a story by Eros Keith
Pictures by Terrence Meagher

Rrra-ah was in his favorite place, on top of a big white clover. He could see everything, the trees and flowers, and the pond where he was born. As he lifted his head, he could feel the summer breeze.

Rrra-ah stuck his nose into a pink clover. He closed his eyes and took a deep breath.

173

He opened his eyes. It was dark!
The sun has fallen, he thought. Then
he heard voices calling, "Look over
here! I've got one!" And Rrra-ah
knew what had happened.

The sun hadn't fallen. He had been
caught!

Rrra-ah saw three children. *Boak! How big and ugly they are!* he thought.

"Ugh! Is he ugly!" said one of the girls. "I think he's cute," said the boy. "He's just a baby," the other girl said.

It was a long way from Rrra-ah's meadow to the children's house. He had been dumped into a big glass jar. Rrra-ah sat very still and watched his pond get smaller and smaller.

"Do you think Mother will let you keep him?"

I hope not! thought Rrra-ah.

"What are you going to call him?"

Rrra-ah called his name as loud as he could.

"Frog—just Frog," said the girl with the jar.

Frog! I'm not a frog! thought Rrra-ah.
I'm a toad and my name is Rrra-ah.

"Mother, look! We found a frog!"

Rrra-ah! Rrra-ah! croaked Rrra-ah.

"Well, you didn't find him in the bathtub," said Mother. "You'll have to find another place to keep him."

Oh, no! thought Rrra-ah. *They are going to keep me!*

One girl brought a box. One girl brought some grass. And the boy brought Rrra-ah turtle food.

Rrra-ah didn't like the box or the turtle food. He didn't eat. He didn't sleep. *I'm not a frog,* he kept thinking. *And I'm not a turtle either!*

In the morning one girl said, "Frog, are you ready to play games with us?"

I'm ready to play escape, thought Rrra-ah, and he leaped from the girl's hands.

He crashed through the living room, the dining room, the hall. And he tipped over three lamps and a vase full of flowers. But he didn't escape. The children caught him.

That night Rrra-ah was very hungry and sad. He heard moths at the window and crickets in the grass. But he couldn't hear the toads by his pond. It was too far away. He didn't sleep because he was thinking about escaping.

The next day Rrra-ah played the escape game again.

"Stop him!" cried Mother. "He's headed for the kitchen!"

SPLAT!

"That does it!" said Mother. "That frog has got to go!"

At last! thought Rrra-ah.

The children carried Rrra-ah back to his meadow. "This is good-bye, Frog," one girl said. "We'll miss your games," said the other. "Maybe we'll see you next summer," said the boy.

Oh, no you won't! thought Rrra-ah. And he was gone.

Then he could see it! His favorite place! He jumped up and there were the trees and the flowers, and the pond where he was born. Rrra-ah stuck his nose into his pink clover, closed his eyes and took a deep breath.

The sun went down behind the trees and from the pond he heard other voices calling, *Rrra-ah. Rrra-ah.*

Questions

1. Why did Rrra-ah think the sun had fallen?

2. What do you think *boak* means in "toad talk"?

3. What food wouldn't Rrra-ah eat?

4. What was Rrra-ah's favorite game?

5. Why was Rrra-ah happy at the end of the story?

6. What can Rrra-ah do if the children come back next summer?

Activity   Write What Happened

Rrra-ah is telling six other toads what happened to him today. He says, "I headed for what they call the kitchen. I could hear them running after me. Then I—"

Finish Rrra-ah's story. Tell or write what Rrra-ah said after that.

You Can't Make a Turtle Come Out

From a song by Malvina Reynolds

You can't make a turtle come out,
You can't make a turtle come out,
You can coax him or call him or shake
    him or shout,
But you can't make a turtle come out,
    come out,
You can't make a turtle come out.

If he wants to stay in his shell,
If he wants to stay in his shell,
You can knock on the door but you
    can't ring the bell,
And you can't make a turtle come out,
    come out,
You can't make a turtle come out.

185

Remarkable Reptiles

Reptiles are animals that have scales and a backbone. Reptiles are coldblooded animals. This means that they have no way to keep their body temperature the same at all times. Reptiles are warm if the place around them is warm. They are cool if the place around them is cool. Because they cannot keep their bodies warm in very cold places, reptiles do not live in the coldest parts of the world.

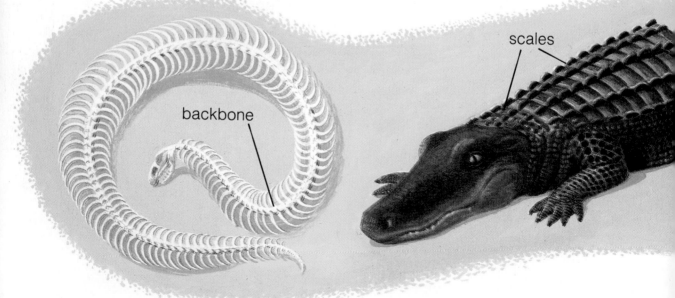

backbone

scales

Pictures by Keith Freeman

Snakes, lizards, turtles, crocodiles, and tuataras (too·uh·TAH·ruhz) make up the five groups of reptiles.

Snakes are the best known group of reptiles. Many snakes are gentle, but some snakes, such as the rattlesnake, can harm you. When the rattlesnake feels something warm coming near, it may bite! It is hard to tell which snakes may harm you. So stay away from snakes.

If you have ever felt the dry, smooth skin of a snake, you may have noticed how cool it feels. You may also have noticed that a snake seems to stare at you. A snake cannot blink because it has no eyelids. It must sleep with its eyes open.

garter snakes

rattlesnake

Lizards make up one of the largest groups of reptiles. There are more than three thousand kinds of lizards. Some make no sound. Others make a squeaking noise.

Lizards are interesting in some other ways, too. Some can lose their tails and grow new ones. One little lizard called a *draco* (DRAY·koh) can sail through the air from tree to tree. A *chameleon* (kuh·MEEL·yuhn) is a lizard that can change its color. This helps it to hide.

draco

chameleons

box turtle

The *turtle* is another reptile that can make a good pet. Turtles can live on land or in water.

The *box turtle* can close its shell tight. If it eats too much, its legs will get too fat to fit inside its shell!

A turtle that lives only on land is called a *tortoise*. Some tortoises can grow big enough to ride. They can weigh as much as two grown people.

tortoises

crocodile

alligator

Crocodiles and alligators are the largest reptiles. They have strong jaws and tails. They use their jaws and tails to help them catch food.

Most reptiles are quiet, but crocodiles and alligators are very noisy. Their song sounds like the grunt of a large hog.

Alligators and crocodiles look very much alike. One way to tell them apart is by looking at their snouts. The crocodile's snout is long and comes to a point. The alligator's snout is shorter and more rounded.

The *tuatara* is the only reptile in its group. It looks like a lizard, except that it has three eyelids.

The tuatara is a strange reptile. It breathes very slowly. Sometimes it does not take a breath for over an hour! The tuatara's eggs hatch slowly, too. The babies do not hatch for at least a year.

A small bird called a *petrel* (PET·ruhl) lives in the same places as the tuatara. The tuatara waits for the petrel to dig a home. Then the tuatara moves in with the little bird. These two seem to like each other's company.

petrel

tuatara

painted turtle

There are many kinds of reptiles in the world. Some of the reptiles may be harmful to people. Some kinds of snakes can give a poisonous bite. Yet many reptiles are useful to people. People in many places in the world eat turtle meat and the meat of large lizards and frogs. The poison of some snakes has been used to make medicine. Reptiles also help people by eating rats, mice, and harmful insects.

Reptiles are remarkable!

Questions

1. Which word does *not* tell about reptiles?
   scales   fur   backbone

2. Which reptiles cannot blink their eyes?

3. Which two reptiles make loud noises?

4. What does it mean when you say that reptiles are *coldblooded?*
   a. Reptiles have cold blood.
   b. Their body temperatures change to fit the place around them.
   c. Reptiles like cold food.

5. Which reptile would you like to have for a pet? Tell why.

Activity   Write Snake Words

Here are some words that tell how a snake's skin feels. The letters curve up and down to look like a snake.

SMOOTH DRY COOL SOFT

Write words that tell how a snake looks. Write the words in a snake shape.

193

Three Little Animals

Poems by Ernesto Galarza

A ciencia cierta
el renacuajo
será mañana
una rana.

*It's a scientific fact
that a frog
is a grown-up
pollywog.*

Lombriz soterrada
trabaja, trabaja
callada, callada.

*An earthworm doesn't
make a sound
when he's working
underground.*

Pictures by Pat Welch and Michael Dowdall

195

Una vez era
una abeja mielera
en panal de cera.

Bees won't bother you.
Relax.
They are busy
making wax.

About ERNESTO GALARZA

Did you ever watch a bee walk across the face of a flower? Did you ever listen to waves booming on the shore? As a boy in Mexico, Ernesto Galarza spent many hours watching and listening to nature.

He says, "We had no radio or television or movies. We had Nature. . . . We learned to use all our senses to hear, feel, smell, and taste all of Nature's performance around us. . . . We put all this together in ways that pleased our fancy. We were poets. Many, many years after I had left my village I tried to remember how we made poetry. And I still try."

More Books by Ernesto Galarza

Spiders in the House
Poemas pe-que pe-que pe-que-nitos (Little Poems)
Rimas tontas (Nutty Rhymes)
Zoo-risa (Fun at the Zoo)

Learn About

Animals in the Library

Make a list of the four books Fred will choose. Write *Storybooks* at the top of the list. Make a list of the four books Sue will choose. Write *Fact Books* at the top.

Pictures by Ed Taber

Choose a book for each animal.

Dinosaur Time

From the story by Peggy Parish

Pictures by Larry Mikec

Long, long ago
the world was different.
More land was under water.
It was warm all the time.
And dinosaurs were everywhere. . . .

There were big dinosaurs.
There were small ones.
There were fast dinosaurs
and slow ones.
Some dinosaurs ate meat.
Some ate plants.

This dinosaur was a giant.
But its mouth was tiny.
It ate plants.
It ate, and ate, and ate
to fill up its big body.
Its name is Brontosaurus
(BRON·tuh·SAWR·us).

This dinosaur was small.
It was as big as a cat.
But it could run fast.
It could catch other animals
and eat them.
Its name is Compsognathus
(comp·SOG·nuh·thus).

This dinosaur was fat.
It was too fat to run from enemies.
That is why it stayed in the water.
It was safe there,
and food was close by.
It ate plants.
Its name is Brachiosaurus
(BRAK·ee·oh·SAWR·us).

This dinosaur was a plant-eater.
It had five horns.
Its name is Pentaceratops
(PEN·tuh·SEHR·uh·tops).
This name is just right.
It means "five-horns-on-the-face."

This dinosaur
was the biggest meat-eater.
Its jaws were huge.
Its teeth were six inches long.
It ate other dinosaurs.
Its name is Tyrannosaurus
(tih·RAN·uh·SAWR·us).

Dinosaurs lived everywhere
for a long time.
Then they died.
Nobody knows why.
But once it was their world.
It was dinosaur time.

Author's Note

We do not know much about dinosaurs. No one ever saw a dinosaur.

But people have found dinosaur fossils, such as footprints, bones, and teeth. Scientists study them, and can tell how big the dinosaurs were, what they ate, and other things about the way they lived.

Scientists learn more each year. But we may never know all about dinosaurs.

Questions

1. Who will win a race?
   Brachiosaurus   Compsognathus

2. Who will hide in the water?
   Brontosaurus   Brachiosaurus

3. Who will eat a flower?
   Brontosaurus   Tyrannosaurus

4. Who has a name with "five" in it?
   Compsognathus   Pentaceratops

5. If you were a Compsognathus, which dinosaur would you *not* like to meet? Tell why not.
   Brontosaurus   Tyrannosaurus

Activity   Write About Dinosaurs

Find a book about dinosaurs. In the book find two dinosaurs that are different from the ones in this story. Write their names and something interesting about each one.

Ultrasaurus

This dinosaur was 100 feet long and weighed 80 tons.

Learn About

"How" and "Why" Stories

People have always wondered about the world. They have wondered how the elephant got its trunk. They have wondered why the sun and the moon are in the sky. Long ago, people made up stories to explain these things. These ''how'' and ''why'' stories came from many lands. This one is from West Africa.

How Spider Got a Bald Head

209

Write or draw your own "how" or "why" story. Tell why an animal looks a certain way, or tell why something happens in nature. Choose one of these story titles, or make up your own title.

Why the Turtle Hides in Its Shell
How Frogs Lost Their Tails
Why There Is Thunder and Lightning

BOOKSHELF

How Puppies Grow by Millicent E. Selsam. Four Winds Press, 1971. Six little puppies are growing up day by day, week by week. What they eat, what they do, and what they learn is shown in photographs.

Millions of Cats by Wanda Gág. Coward-McCann, 1928. An old woman and an old man want one cat to care for. What will they do with the millions of cats that show up at their door?

Ji-Nongo-Nongo Means Riddles by Verna Aardema. Four Winds Press, 1978. These riddles come from many places in Africa. Some of the riddles are about animals. Others are about the jobs people have.

The Carsick Zebra and Other Animal Riddles by Tomie dePaola. Holiday House, 1983. A book of animal riddles. The pictures are as fun to look at as the riddles are to solve.

Little Raccoon and Poems from the Woods by Lilian Moore. McGraw-Hill, 1975. A collection of poems about the wonderful creatures around.

5 Long, Long Ago

Heart of the Woods

A poem by Wesley Curtright

Deep into the woods we'll go,
Hand in hand.
Let the woods close about us,
Let the world outside be lost—
And let us find that Secret City
Lost so long ago—
In the Heart of the Woods.

Picture by Christa Kieffer

The Magic Porridge Pot

A German folk tale retold by Paul Galdone

Pictures by Jane Teiko Oka

Once upon a time, long, long ago, a girl and her mother lived in a small house at the end of the village. They were very poor. Often they had nothing to eat but a small piece of bread.

When there was no food in the house, the girl would go into the forest to look for nuts and berries. One morning she could not find a single nut or berry.

At last she sat down and started to cry.

"There's no food for Mother and me. What will we do? We're so hungry."

"Cheer up, my dear," said a friendly voice.

The girl looked up in surprise. She saw a woman who wore a long cloak and leaned on a crooked stick.

"Do not worry, my dear," said the woman. "You will never be hungry again."

From under her cloak she took out a small black pot.

"This is a magic pot, my dear. Put it on the fire. Say to it,

'Boil, Little Pot, boil!'

and at once it will fill up with delicious porridge. When you have had all you can eat, say to it,

'Stop, Little Pot, stop!'

Then the magic pot will stop boiling."

"Oh, thank you so much," said the girl.

"Never forget the magic words, my dear," said the woman. "Never forget!" And no sooner had she said this than she disappeared.

The girl carried the pot home as fast
as she could run.

"What have you got?" her mother asked
when she saw the pot.

"This is a magic pot that will cook
delicious porridge," the girl answered.
"A woman in the forest gave it to me."

The girl was eager to try out the magic
pot. She set it on the fire and said,

"Boil, Little Pot, boil!"

Sure enough, delicious porridge bubbled
up.

When they had had all that they could
eat, the girl said,

   "Stop, Little Pot, stop!"
and the magic pot stopped boiling.

For a long time the girl and her mother
had as much porridge as they wanted. They
were very happy.

Then one day the girl went to visit her
friend at the other end of the village.
She was gone a long while and her mother
began to be hungry. So she set the magic
pot on the fire and said to it,

   "Boil, Little Pot, boil!"
The porridge began to fill the pot, and
the mother dished out a nice bowlful.

Soon the porridge was bubbling at the top of the pot. But the mother had forgotten the magic words. The porridge kept on coming. It began to spill over the top.

"Halt, Little Pot, halt!" the mother said.

The porridge only boiled and bubbled over faster.

"Enough, Little Pot, enough!" cried the mother, trying to remember the right words.

The porridge went right on bubbling over. Soon it covered the floor of the cottage.

The mother struggled to the door and opened it wide to let the porridge out of the house.

"No more, Little Pot, no more!" she shouted.

The stream of porridge ran through the cottage door and onto the street. Down the street ran the mother crying, **"Cease, Little Pot, cease!"** But the porridge went on and on, toward the very last house in the village where the girl was visiting.

When the mother came to the house she called, "Help, help! The magic pot keeps boiling, boiling, boiling!"

At once the girl guessed what was
wrong. So she waded into the thick, heavy
porridge and ran home as fast as she could,
with her mother behind her.

When the girl reached the cottage she
cried,

"Stop, Little Pot, stop!
  Stop, Little Pot, stop!
Stop, Little Pot, stop!
  Stop, Little Pot, stop!"

And the magic pot stopped boiling.

Then everyone in the village came out
into the street carrying dippers, spoons,
cups, bowls, and buckets. They dipped up
the porridge, and they scooped up the
porridge, and they spooned up the porridge.
There was enough porridge for everyone to
eat for days and days.

After that, the girl and her mother
and the people of the village never went
hungry. And they never forgot the words
to stop the magic pot from boiling.

Questions

1. What did the mother forget?

2. Why did the girl say, "Stop, Little Pot, stop!" four times instead of just once?

3. Which word best tells about the pot?
    silly   magic   black

4. Pretend you are a person who lives in the village. Are you glad or sorry that the mother forgot the magic words? Tell why you are glad or sorry that she forgot them.

5. Three of these words mean almost the same as *stop.* Which three?
    halt   enough   crooked
    boil   nothing   cease

Activity   Write Magic Words

Here is a magic box. Write the magic words that make the box work. Draw or write what happens when you say your magic words.

Some One

A poem by Walter de la Mare

Some one came knocking
   At my wee, small door;
Some one came knocking,
   I'm sure—sure—sure;
I listened, I opened,
   I looked to left and right,
But nought there was a-stirring
   In the still dark night;
Only the busy beetle
   Tap-tapping in the wall,
Only from the forest
   The screech-owl's call,
Only the cricket whistling
   While the dewdrops fall,
So I know not who came knocking,
   At all, at all, at all.

Picture by Judith Gwyn Brown

The Trolls and the Pussy Cat

Adapted from the Norwegian folk tale retold by George Jonsen

Pictures by Kinuko Craft

There was once a hunter who lived in the far north. One day he caught a big white bear. He had never seen a bear so big and so white and so tame. I will take this bear to the king, he thought.

But soon the snow began to fall. The wind began to blow. The hunter was very cold. He stopped at a small house and knocked at the door.

The door opened right away. There stood a farmer and his family all dressed in heavy coats and boots.

"May I stay the night with you?" asked the hunter. "The snow and ice have frozen my poor bear and me."

"Ah! You would not want to stay in
this house," said the farmer. "The trolls
will be coming down the mountain tonight.
They eat our food. They sleep in our
beds. We are lucky if they don't break
all our dishes and tables and chairs."

"We are going to leave," said the
farmer's wife. "We are going to sleep in
a cave in the woods."

"Wait!" said the hunter. "Don't go.
Let my bear and me stay here with you.
Maybe we can help you."

So the bear crawled under the table. The hunter lay down on the floor with a blanket. And the farmer's family went to sleep in their own beds.

They did not sleep for long. Soon there was a loud noise outside the door.

"Farmer Neils! Farmer Neils! We have come for our dinner. Open the door and let us in."

The door flew open and in ran the
trolls. They ran into the kitchen. They
pulled out the dishes. They carried out
great bowls of food and began eating it.

Suddenly a little troll looked under
the table. He saw the bear's white nose.
"Look here!" he called. "I see a pussy
cat! Nice pussy cat!"

He put some hot meat on a long stick.
He poked it at the bear's nose.

With a roar, the bear jumped out, picked up the troll, and threw him right out the door.

You never saw such a thing! Trolls were running out the door. Trolls were jumping out the windows. One even climbed up the chimney!

The next morning the hunter and his bear set off to see the king. Before long everyone had heard about Farmer Neils and his big pussy cat. And from that day on no more trolls came to visit his house.

Questions

1. What were Farmer Neils and his family afraid of?

2. How do you think Farmer Neils knew that the trolls were coming that night?

3. At first, the trolls had a great time in the house. What changed all that?

4. What do you think happened to the bear after the story ended?

5. Which word tells the most about the story? Why?

       scary   funny   sad   true

6. Which word tells *why* the hunter was not afraid of the bear?

       big   cold   tame

Activity   Write What Happened

Be one of the trolls who visited Farmer Neils's house. Write what happened to you. What did you say and do when you got home?

Socks for Supper

A story by Jack Kent

Pictures by Justin Wager

In a faraway place in a long-ago time there lived an old man and his wife. They were very poor. All they had was a tumble-down house and a tiny turnip garden.

One day, the man said to his wife, "One can get tired of eating nothing but turnips."

Not far away there lived a couple who had a cow.

The old man and his wife used to look at the cow and dream of milk and cheese.

"Maybe they'll sell us some," said the old man.

"We don't have any money," his wife reminded him.

"Perhaps we could trade them something for some milk," said the old man.

"Perhaps we could," his wife agreed. And they searched the house for something to trade.

They looked and looked, but the only thing they could find that wasn't in pieces or tatters was a pair of socks.

The old man took the socks and went
to see the couple who had the cow.

A little while later he came happily
home again with a bucket of milk and a
small cheese.

"Oh! This is so good!" said his wife.

It wasn't long before they began to
wish they had some more. But they didn't
have any more socks to trade.

"I will knit some!" said the old woman.
But she didn't have any yarn.

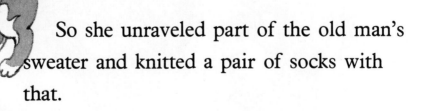

So she unraveled part of the old man's sweater and knitted a pair of socks with that.

They again traded the socks for milk
and cheese. And they feasted as they did
before.

When it was all gone, the old woman
knitted another pair of socks. And once
more the old man traded them for milk
and cheese.

When that was gone, the old woman started knitting again. But there was now only enough yarn left for one sock.

"What good is one sock?" the old woman asked. "They won't trade any milk or cheese for that."

"We'll see," said the old man. And he took the sock to the couple with the cow.

"I only have half a pair of socks this time," he said. "Would you trade half a bucket of milk and half a cheese for this?"

"Oh, no, that is not necessary," said the farmer.

"You see," said the farmer's wife, "One sock is exactly what I need."

She was knitting her husband a sweater
for his birthday. She'd gotten the yarn for
it by unraveling the socks and she needed
just one more to finish the job.

But the sweater didn't fit. So the wife gave it to the old man, for she had noticed he didn't have one. And it was just the right size.

Questions

1. What was traded in the story?

2. How many socks were in this story?

3. How many sweaters were in this story?

4. What did the old woman do to the old man's sweater?
   - **a.** She unraveled it.
   - **b.** She knit it for supper.
   - **c.** She sold it.
   - **d.** She made it into a coat.

5. Why is the story called "Socks for Supper"?

6. What do you think happened after the story was over?

Activity Write a Story

The cow wanted something. She traded something to get what she wanted. Tell or write what the cow wanted. Tell or write what she traded. Tell or write a story about what happened.

Alarm Clock

A poem by Eve Merriam

in the deep sleep forest
there were ferns
there were feathers
there was fur
and a soft ripe peach
on a branch within my

r–r–r–r–r–r–r–r–r–r–r–r–r

Picture by Kinuko Craft

BOOKSHELF

Strega Nona retold by Tomie dePaola. Prentice-Hall, 1975. Strega Nona is a wise old woman with magic powers. Big Anthony helps her with her house and garden until he becomes more interested in finding out how Strega Nona's magic pasta pot works.

Why the Sun and the Moon Live in the Sky by Elphinstone Dayrell. Houghton Mifflin, 1968. Long ago sun, moon, and water all lived on the earth. Sun and moon wanted their friend water to visit, but water with all his people couldn't fit in their house.

The Fire Stealer retold by William Toye. Oxford University Press, 1980. Nanabozho uses magic to bring fire to his people.

Monster Tracks? by A. Delaney. Harper & Row, 1981. Walking through the woods, a little boy sees some tracks. He thinks it is evidence that a monster is following him.

The Nose Tree by Warwick Hutton. Atheneum, 1981. Three soldiers share their campfire with a stranger. In return, they receive magic gifts.

6 We Could Be Friends

We Could Be Friends

A poem by Myra Cohn Livingston

We could be friends
Like friends are supposed to be.
You, picking up the telephone
Calling me

   to come over and play
   or take a walk,
   finding a place
   to sit and talk,

Or just goof around
Like friends do,
Me, picking up the telephone
Calling you.

Picture by Susan Lexa

257

The Traveling Musicians

A play based on the German folk tale collected by the Brothers Grimm

Pictures by Willi K. Baum

Characters

Storyteller 1	**Dog**	**Robber 1**
Storyteller 2	**Rooster**	**Robber 2**
Donkey	**Cat**	**Robber 3**

Storyteller 1: Once there was a donkey who had worked for his master for many years. At last he grew too old to carry wheat to the mill. His master did not want him any more.

Donkey: My body is weak, but my voice is still strong. I think I will go to the town of Bremen and sing for my living.

Storyteller 2: So the donkey ran away. On the way to Bremen he met a dog. She was lying by the side of the road panting.

Donkey: Why are you out of breath?

Dog: I ran away from my master. He no longer wants me because I am too old to hunt with him. What shall I do now?

Donkey: You may as well come with me, my friend. We will go to Bremen and sing for our living.

Storyteller 1: So the two went on down the road. Before long they met a cat. He was sitting in the middle of the road looking very sad.

Donkey: Why are you so sad, old cat?

Cat: Ah me! My poor old teeth are not as sharp as they used to be. And I'd rather sit by the fire than run after mice. No one wants me, so I'm running away.

Donkey: Come with us to Bremen. The dog and I are going to be musicians. We can all make music together.

Storyteller 2: That made the cat happy, and he went along with the donkey and the dog. After a while they came to a farm. A rooster flew up onto the gate and crowed.

Donkey: What is this noise about? Is something the matter?

Rooster: Cock-a-doodle-doo! This is probably my last crow. For years I woke everyone up in the morning. Now I hear they are planning to make me into soup!

Donkey: What a fine voice you have! Don't stay here and have your head cut off! Come with us! We are going to Bremen to sing for our living. With your voice we shall all make good money.

Storyteller 1:　So the four friends went on their way. When night came, they stopped by a big tree to rest.

Storyteller 2:　The donkey and the dog lay down under the tree. The cat climbed up into the branches. And the rooster flew to the top of the tree, where he could see all around. Before the others could go to sleep, the rooster called to them.

Rooster: I see lights over there. It must be a house.

Donkey: Let's go there. It will be better than sleeping under this tree.

Dog: And we may find something to eat.

Storyteller 1: So the rooster led them all to the house.

Storyteller 2: When they reached the house, the donkey went to the window. Being the biggest, he could stretch his neck just enough to look inside.

Dog: Well, what do you see?

Donkey: I see three robbers sitting at a table. They are eating dinner. The food looks delicious!

Cat: I would like some of that food. How do you think we might get some?

Rooster: Perhaps together we can think of a plan to frighten away the robbers.

Storyteller 1: So the animals talked together and decided what to do. The donkey kept his place near the window. The dog climbed on the donkey's back. The cat climbed on the dog's back. The rooster flew up to the cat's head. Then they began their music.

All together: Hee—Haaaw! Arf! Arf—arf—arf! Meooow-w-w! Meooow-w-w! Cock-a-doodle-dooo-o!

Storyteller 2: The sound of that music badly frightened the robbers. They ran out the door and into the woods crying,

Three Robbers: Run for your life! Goblins are after us!

Storyteller 1: When the robbers were gone, the donkey, the dog, the cat, and the rooster went into the house and had a good dinner. Then they all found places to sleep. The cat curled up by the fireplace. The dog lay down beside the door. The donkey stretched out in the yard. The rooster flew to the rooftop. They soon fell fast asleep.

Storyteller 2: About midnight, the robbers came back. The house was dark. Everything was quiet.

Storyteller 1: So one robber went inside to look around. First he went into the kitchen. He saw two bright lights on the floor, and he thought they were coals from the fire.

Robber 1: I'll light a match by this fire. Then I'll be able to see better.

Storyteller 2: But when he bent down, the cat jumped and scratched him on the hand. The robber cried out with fear. He ran to get out the door. There the dog bit the robber in the leg. As he rushed into the yard, the robber was given a big kick by the donkey. Then the rooster woke up and crowed.

Rooster: Cock-a-doodle-doo-o!
Cock-a-doodle-doo-o!

Storyteller 1: The robber ran quickly to tell the others what happened.

Robber 1:   Run! Run! The goblins almost killed me! A goblin with long fingernails scratched my hand! Another one cut me in the leg with a knife! Then a big goblin kicked me and knocked me down while a goblin on the roof kept shouting, "Cook him in a stew! Cook him in a stew!"

Storyteller 2:   The robbers lost no time in running far away. This time they didn't come back. As for the donkey, the dog, the cat, and the rooster, they lived together in that house for a long, long time.

Questions

1. Why is this play called "The Traveling Musicians"?

2. The robbers heard sounds outside their house. Who was there?

3. One robber saw two lights. What were the lights?

4. One robber said he heard a goblin shout, "Cook him in a stew." What had he really heard?

5. Do you think that the four animals should have gone on to Bremen? Why or why not?

Activity **Write a Jobs List**

How might the four animals keep house together? How might they share the work? Make a **JOBS** list. Write or draw what each animal should do to help keep house.

JOBS

Cat
1. sweep
2.
3.
Donkey
1.
2.

271

The four friends in *The Traveling Musicians* traveled the road to Bremen. This story map shows the road and some places along the way.

272

Match each sentence below with a
place on the story map. Use the letters
on the map for answers.

1. The donkey ran away from this place.

2. The donkey met the dog here.

3. The rooster sang his last
   "Cock-a-doodle-doo" for his master.

4. The four musicians rested here.

5. The donkey and the dog met the cat
   near this spot.

6. Robbers once lived here.

7. The four musicians never reached
   this place.

8. The four musicians live here now.

The Elves and the Shoemaker

Adapted from the German folk tale collected by
the Brothers Grimm

Pictures by Gene Sharp

Once there lived a fine shoemaker who became very poor. At last, he had only enough leather to make one pair of shoes.

As he cut the leather, the shoemaker looked sadly at his wife.

"Dear wife," he said, "I'm tired. I'll make these shoes tomorrow."

He laid the leather pieces on his work table. Then he went to bed.

The next day the shoemaker found a beautiful pair of shoes on the table!

"Oh, my!" said the surprised shoemaker. "Who could have made these shoes?"

The shoemaker looked closely at the shoes. They were stitched together perfectly.

Later that day a man came into the shop to buy a pair of shoes. The shoemaker showed the man the only pair he had. The man put on the shoes. They were a perfect fit! The man was so pleased with the shoes that he paid extra money for them.

"Dear wife," said the shoemaker. "Now I have enough money to buy leather for TWO pairs of shoes."

That night the shoemaker cut the leather for two pairs of shoes. He left the pieces on his work table.

"I'll make the shoes in the morning," he said. Then he went to bed.

But in the morning the shoemaker found two pairs of shoes on the table!

"Oh, my!" said the surprised shoemaker. "*Who* could have made these shoes?"

"I don't know," said his wife. "But they're perfect in every way!"

Two people came into the shop. They bought two pairs of shoes. Each of them gave the shoemaker a fine price, too.

"Dear wife," said the shoemaker that night. "I made good money today. Now I have enough leather for FOUR pairs of shoes!"

The happy shoemaker cut the leather and left the pieces on his work table for the night.

And what do you think the shoemaker found in the morning?

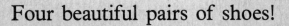

Four beautiful pairs of shoes!

The same thing happened again and again. Each night the shoemaker cut the leather for the shoes. Each morning he found the shoes already made. The shoes were always perfect. And the shoemaker made more and more money.

Then one night the shoemaker said, "Dear wife, let's stay up tonight. Let's see who is helping us."

So that night the shoemaker and his wife hid in a dark corner of the shop.

When the clock struck midnight, the door of the shop flew open. In tumbled two elves dressed in tattered clothes. They went to work at once on the shoes.

The elves sang happily as they worked.

"Snip the leather.

Sew a stitch.

Make a fine shoe—

Tip, tap, tap, tip!"

Soon the elves had made all of the shoes. Then they ran out of the shop.

The shoemaker's wife turned to him and said, "Dear husband, those little elves have helped us so much. I think we should do something for them. I'll make them some new clothes. And you'll make them two fine pairs of shoes!"

"What a wonderful idea!" said the shoemaker. "Let's begin in the morning."

All the next day the couple worked. The shoemaker's wife made two little pairs of pants, two little shirts, and two little vests. She made two little pairs of socks and two fine little hats. The shoemaker made two perfect little pairs of shoes.

That night they laid the clothes on the table. Then they hid in a dark corner of the shop.

When the clock struck midnight, the door of the shop flew open. In tumbled the elves. They jumped onto the table—and then they saw the clothes. Their eyes grew wide with delight. They danced up and down and giggled with glee.

The elves put on their new clothes.
Everything was a perfect fit!

They danced and sang a new song.

   "What handsome little elves are we,
    No longer shoemakers will we be!"

They hopped and danced around the
room and out the door. The shoemaker and
his wife never saw them again.

But from then on life always went well
for the shoemaker and his wife.

Questions

1. What did the elves do to help the shoemaker?

2. What did the shoemaker and his wife do to help the elves?

3. If the elves came to help you, what two things would you ask them to do?

4. If you helped the elves, what two things would you do for them?

5. Could "The Elves and the Shoemaker" really happen? Why or why not?

6. The elves *tumbled* and *jumped.* Write three other words ending in *–ed* that tell what the elves did. Find the words in the story.

Activity   Write a List

Think of all the different kinds of shoes that people wear. Make a list of everyday shoes, sport shoes, and other shoes.

283

CONNECTIONS

A Sneaker Factory

Long ago, shoes were made by hand with hand tools. It took one day, or more, to make a pair of shoes. Most of the shoes were made from leather. They were sewed together by hand.

Now, shoes are made by machines in factories. Many workers work on one pair of shoes. Many pairs of shoes can be made in one day.

This is the old way shoes were made—by hand.

284

Pictures by Tom Dunnington

This is a sneaker factory. When the sneakers are made, the bottom part of the shoe comes first.

A flat piece of rubber is put on a hot machine. The machine presses the rubber. Then the rubber looks like the bottom of a sneaker. The bottom part is called the *sole*.

This is the way new sneakers are made in a factory. The bottoms come first.

The top part of the sneaker comes next. Cloth is rolled out onto a large table and cut. Many layers of the cloth are piled on top of one another. Workers set a sneaker pattern on top of the pile. Then they swing a sharp metal cutting tool above the cloth. One worker pushes a button. The fabric is cut.

Stitchers sew the cloth for the left and right sides together. They sew them up the back. The stitchers make the shoe look fancy. They sew a star, a bolt of lightning, or another design on the side of the shoe.

A machine sews a leather piece where the shoelaces will go. Then holes are cut in the leather for the shoelaces.

Now they are sewing on the stars, one by one. I <u>love</u> stars.

The tongue, the toe, and the heel of the sneaker are then cut out of the cloth. The tongue is sewed to the cloth side. Next, a worker sews the toe piece and the heel to the sneaker.

Workers hang the sneakers on a rack. The sneakers are ready for the next step.

The sneaker is put in a hot machine.
The machine shapes the shoe like a foot.

Then the workers sand the sneakers
until the bottoms are smooth.

The sole and the top part of the sneaker
are put together next. A special type of
glue is brushed on the sneakers to hold
them together.

Then they shape them and sand them and glue them together.

When the sneakers are finished, the shoelaces are put in. Then workers put the shoes into boxes. The boxes are sent to stores around the world. People will buy the sneakers from the stores.

Which pair would you like to buy?

Finally, they send the sneakers to stores. I bought my sneakers in this store. I love them.

Questions

1. Look at the mixed-up pictures. What is the order for making sneakers?

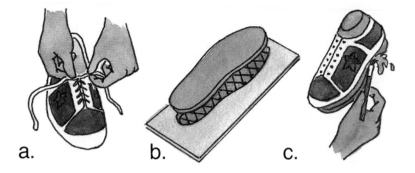

a.

b.

c.

2. Who will use each pair of shoes?

a.

b.

c.

ballet slippers   sandals   rubber boots

Activity   Draw and Write About Magic Shoes

Think of a pair of magic shoes. Draw a picture of your magic shoes. Tell what they can do.

Split Pea Soup

Story and pictures by James Marshall

Martha was very fond of making split pea soup. Sometimes she made it all day long. Pots and pots of split pea soup.

If there was one thing that George was *not* fond of, it was split pea soup. As a matter of fact, George hated split pea soup more than anything else in the world. But it was so hard to tell Martha.

One day after George had eaten ten bowls of Martha's soup, he said to himself, "I just can't stand another bowl. Not even another spoonful."

So, while Martha was out in the kitchen, George carefully poured the rest of his soup into his loafers under the table. "Now she will think I have eaten it."

But Martha was watching from the kitchen.

"How do you expect to walk home with your loafers full of split pea soup?" she asked George.

"Oh, dear," said George. "You saw me."

"And why didn't you tell me that you hate my split pea soup?"

"I didn't want to hurt your feelings," said George.

"That's silly," said Martha. "Friends should always tell each other the truth. As a matter of fact, I don't like split pea soup very much myself. I only like to make it. From now on, you'll never have to eat that awful soup again."

"What a relief!" George sighed.

"Would you like some chocolate chip cookies instead?" asked Martha.

"Oh, that would be lovely," said George.

"Then you shall have them," said his friend.

297

Questions

1. "George, why don't you like split pea soup?" Answer for George.

2. "Martha, why did you try to give George eleven bowls of split pea soup?" Answer for Martha.

3. "George, what do you wear on your feet when you go to visit Martha?" Answer for George.

4. "Martha, what will you cook for George the next time he eats at your house?" Answer for Martha.

Activity   **Write Words for a Play**

Finish the play. Your friend wants you to do something you don't want to do. What does your friend say? What will you answer? Write as much as you wish.

Friend: I want you to _____.
Me: _____.

From

Grandfather

A poem by Shirley Crawford

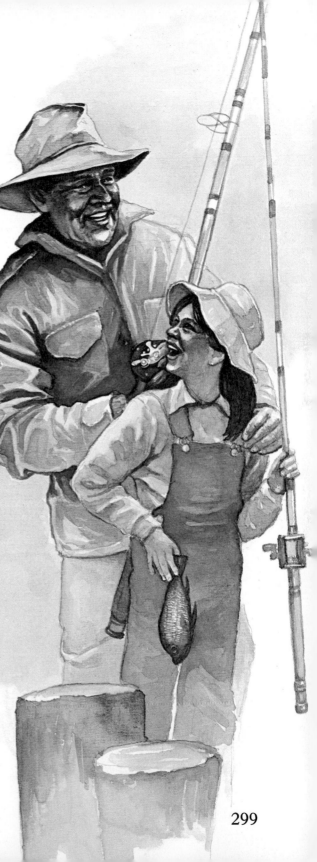

Grandfather sings, I dance.
Grandfather speaks, I listen.
Now I sing, who will dance?
I speak, who will listen?

Grandfather hunts, I learn.
Grandfather fishes, I clean.
Now I hunt, who will learn?
I fish, who will clean?

Picture by Konrad Hack

Crystal Is the New Girl

Adapted from the story by Shirley Gordon
Pictures by Dora Leder

Crystal is the new girl in our school. We all stare at her when she comes into class. Nobody in school is friends with Crystal. Crystal acts like she doesn't care.

The teacher tells Crystal to sit next to me. "I hope you and Crystal will learn to be friends, Susan," the teacher tells me. I don't want to learn to be Crystal's friend.

"What's your name? What's your name?"
Crystal keeps asking me.

"You know my name is Susan," I keep
telling her.

"I just want to make sure you don't
catch *amnesia*," Crystal says.

Crystal smiles, but I don't smile back.

The teacher tells Crystal and me to *Hush!*

"The teacher was cross," I tell my mother after school, "because Crystal was talking to me in class."

"Who is Crystal?" my mother asks.

"Crystal is the new girl in school," I explain.

"Oh, it's nice you have a new friend."

"Crystal isn't my friend," I tell my mother.

Crystal is wearing her sunglasses in class. She doesn't want to take them off. "I can see New York with them," says Crystal.

"No, you can't," I tell her.

Crystal smiles at me and says, "San Francisco?"

I try not to smile, but I can't help it.

"Shhhh!" The teacher looks down his nose at Crystal and me.

"The teacher was cross again," I tell my mother after school, "because Crystal was talking to me in class."

"Crystal shouldn't talk in class," my mother tells me.

"Crystal says funny things," I tell my mother.

Crystal and I are taking a test. Crystal whispers at me, "Don't let me see your paper. That would be cheating."

I make a face at Crystal, and she makes a face back at me.

The teacher shakes his head at us and says, "Ah-ah-ah!"

"Crystal and I were sent to the principal's office today," I tell my mother after school.

"You and Crystal shouldn't get into so much trouble."

"Crystal and I are friends," I tell my mother.

Crystal rolls up her paper like a telescope. She holds it up to her eye and squints through it at the sun outside the window. "It's time for lunch," Crystal says.

The teacher looks at us. Then he looks at his watch and says, "It's time for lunch."

Crystal and I sit on the playground and open our lunch boxes. Crystal's lunch is bologna and mine is peanut butter and jelly.

"I'll trade you half of mine for half of yours," says Crystal.

307

"Crystal and I shared our lunch today," I tell my mother after school.

"That's nice."

"Crystal and I are going to be friends forever," I tell my mother.

"*Sss-sss!*" Crystal hisses at me like a snake.

"Shhh," I tell her. "We can't talk in class."

"Snakes don't talk," says Crystal. Crystal giggles, and I giggle with her.

The teacher clucks his tongue at us and makes a noise like *Tsk-tsk-tsk!*

"The teacher won't let Crystal and me sit together anymore," I tell my mother after school.

"That's too bad."

"Crystal and I are still friends," I tell my mother.

It is summer, and the last day of school. I look across the room at Crystal. She is wearing two new hair ribbons. One is red and one is green. Crystal smiles at me and calls out, "Merry Christmas!"

The teacher looks at us and says, "Class dismissed."

My mother takes a picture of Crystal and me for my scrapbook. Then Crystal's mother comes to drive her home.

"I wish Crystal lived next door to us," I tell my mother.

"You'll see Crystal again when school starts in the fall."

Crystal's face in the car window gets smaller and smaller.

"Don't catch amnesia and forget me!" hollers Crystal.

I wish there was school tomorrow.

Questions

1. Why didn't Susan want to be Crystal's friend?

2. What two things changed Susan's mind about being Crystal's friend?

3. When the teacher "looks down his nose" at Crystal and Susan, he is
   a. having amnesia
   b. looking down a telescope
   c. feeling cross

4. Do you think that Susan and Crystal should sit together at school? Why or why not?

5. Why did Susan say, "I wish there was school tomorrow"?

6. What do you think happened to Susan and Crystal the next year?

Activity   Write Ways to Welcome Someone

A new person has come to your class. Write three things you might do to make that person feel welcome.

Spinning Song

A poem by Zilpha Keatley Snyder

The bar is smooth
    beneath our knees,
Our hands are strong,
    we sit at ease,
And when we're set
    we grab hold tight,
And back we spin
    with all our might.
The bar gets hot—
    around, around—
Our flying hair
    whips air and ground.
Of all who spin
    on playground bars,
We are the best!
    we are the stars!
Jeanette's my friend,
    and it is she,
Who always goes
    around with me.

Picture by Susan Lexa

BOOKSHELF

Best Friends for Frances by Russell Hoban. Harper & Row, 1969. Frances is angry with her best friend Albert. She makes her sister Gloria her best friend and starts to go with her on a picnic. Albert is upset. He wants to go, too.

Nate the Great and the Sticky Case by Marjorie Weinman Sharmat. Coward, McCann & Geoghegan, 1978. Nate tries to help his friend Claude find his lost stegosaurus stamp.

Sugaring Time by Kathryn Lasky. Macmillan, 1983. The people of the countryside are harvesting the sweetness from the trees.

The 329th Friend by Marjorie Weinman Sharmat. Four Winds Press, 1979. After giving a party for 328 animal friends, Emery Raccoon finds another good friend— himself.

The Night After Christmas by James Stevenson. Greenwillow, 1981. A kind-hearted dog rescues two toys from the garbage and helps them find a new home.

Key Words

Dilly Dilly Piccalilli

chap — page 12

Who Ever Sausage a Thing?

sausage — page 13

Pierre: A Cautionary Tale in Five Chapters and a Prologue

suitable — page 14

moral — page 14

shock — page 26

guest — page 30

What Can They Be?

wooden — page 33

mark — page 33

Oh, A-Hunting We Will Go

bunk — page 36

brontosaurus — page 37

chorus — page 37

Solomon Grundy

time machine — page 38

Riding on Two Wheels

bicycle — page 40

"Fire! Fire!"

risky — page 49

alarm — page 49

The Garden

garden — page 50

seed — page 51

Teeny-Tiny

bonnet — page 66

cupboard — page 68

Something Is There

stair — page 71

Grandfather's Story

goblin — page 72

peek — page 78

chuckle — page 82

A Ghost Story

post — page 85

Shadows

shadow — page 86

We Three

between — page 106

At the Top of My Voice

thunders   page 110

rings   page 110

Max

sneakers   page 118

The Ant and the Dove

pity   page 133

raft   page 133

might   page 135

Mary Jo's Grandmother

biscuits   page 141

pantry   page 141

Safety Bear

safety   page 154

ambulance   page 157

Snowflakes Drift

drift   page 160

melting   page 160

Soft Grass

stony   page 162

Rope Rhyme

ground   page 164

Caballito

galloping   page 170

caballito   page 170

Rrra-ah

clover   page 172

meadow   page 175

escape   page 178

crashed   page 179

You Can't Make a Turtle Come Out

coax   page 184

Remarkable Reptiles

reptile   page 186

Three Little Animals

scientific   page 194

fact   page 194

Dinosaur Time

dinosaurs   page 200

LEARN ABOUT STORIES: "How" and "Why" Stories

bald   page 208

Heart of the Woods

heart page 214

The Magic Porridge Pot

porridge page 216

cloak page 218

boil page 219

waded page 225

Some One

a-stirring page 228

The Trolls and the Pussy Cat

trolls page 230

tame page 231

Socks for Supper

tatters page 240

knit page 243

unravel page 244

We Could Be Friends

friend page 256

telephone page 256

The Traveling Musicians

musicians page 258

goblins page 267

stew page 270

LEARN ABOUT STORIES: Follow the Road to Bremen

map page 272

The Elves and the Shoemaker

leather page 274

shop page 275

midnight page 279

tattered page 279

glee page 281

A Sneaker Factory

factory page 285

sneaker page 285

sole page 285

fabric page 286

Split Pea Soup

fond of page 292

split pea soup page 292

loafers page 295

Crystal Is the New Girl

amnesia page 302

telescope page 307

squints page 307

bologna page 307

scrapbook page 310

Spinning Song

at ease page 313

Sounds and Letters

/a/	bat page 123	raft page 133	match page 268
/e/	net page 134	shell page 184	bed page 15
/i/	lips page 160	stick page 235	six page 168
/o/	fox page 34	frog page 51	pot page 216
/u/	skunk page 36	bunk page 36	cup page 226

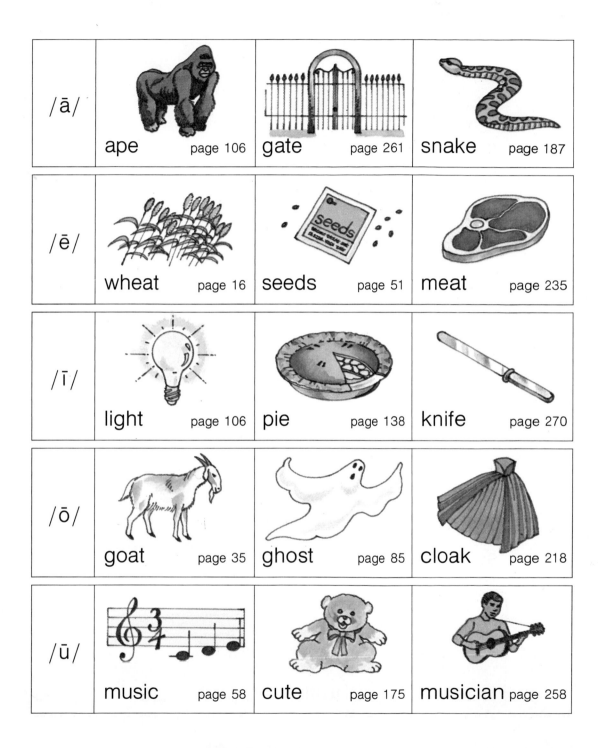

/ā/	ape page 106	gate page 261	snake page 187
/ē/	wheat page 16	seeds page 51	meat page 235
/ī/	light page 106	pie page 138	knife page 270
/ō/	goat page 35	ghost page 85	cloak page 218
/ū/	music page 58	cute page 175	musician page 258

/ar/	car page 148	jar page 175	yarn page 243
/er/	mother page 137	father page 137	water page 200
/ir/	chair page 116	bird page 146	girl page 150
/or/	story page 88	forest page 217	door page 231
/ur/	four page 169	turtle page 184	curb page 158